Creating Residual Internet Income

How to Generate a Life-long Online Income

OLAWALE ONASANYA

www.online-business-success-tips.blogspot.com

TABLE OF CONTENTS

FOREWORD   5

DEDICATION   7

ACKNOWLEDGEMENT   8

INTRODUCTION   GETTING READY TO CREATING RESIDUAL INCOME: The Fundamentals 13

CHAPTER 1   INFORMATION PRODUCTS: Earn Residual Income From Info Products   25

CHAPTER 2   AFFILIATE MARKETING: Make Money By Selling Other People's Products   51

CHAPTER 3   GOOGLE ADSENSE: How To Make Money With Google Adsense   67

CHAPTER 4   MAKE MONEY SELLING YOUR SERVICES: Take Your Services To The Next Level   95

CHAPTER 5   ONLINE AUCTIONS: Make Money Through Online Auctions   109

CHAPTER 6   DIGITAL PHOTOGRAPHS: Make Money Selling Digital Photos   117

CHAPTER 7   DATA ENTRY: Make Money Entering Online Data For Companies   131

CHAPTER 8   MAKE MONEY SELLING PHYSICAL PRODUCTS (HARD GOODS)   139

CHAPTER 9   SELLING ADVERTISING SPACE   151

CHAPTER 10   JOINT VENTURES   157

CHAPTER 11   MAKE MONEY SELLING/OFFERING
INTERNET INFRASTRUCTURES   163

CHAPTER 12   MAKE MONEY WITH INCENTIVE
OFFERS   169

CHAPTER 13   ESSENTIAL ONLINE BUSINESS TOOLS:
Must- Have Internet Tools For Optimal
Results   173

CHAPTER 14   ONLINE TRAFFIC GENERATION: ... Key To
Online Business Success 1   189

CHAPTER 15   OFFLINE TRAFFIC GENERATION: ... Key To
Online Business Success 2   213

CHAPTER 16   OPTING FOR ONLINE BUSINESSES THAT
FIT YOU   219

CHAPTER 17   ...GETTING STARTED RIGHT AWAY   227

FOREWORD

Creating Residual Internet Income is a simple, straight forward book that exposes step by step ways of enhancing your income regardless of your profession or level of once knowledge in computer. Especially important is the tactical way the author leads the reader through the rudiments of various avenues of making money through internet.

Money is a defense and it also answereth all things; it is therefore, impossible for anyone to do without money. With a copy of this book in the palm of your hand, your coast in the area of business you offer can easily and profitably be enlarged by selling your products or rendering your services in every corner of the globe. Your customers or your clients will go beyond your locality.

I strongly believe that all those who will have access to this book will acquire new insight and knowledge on how to improve on their residual income; I, therefore, commend the book to numerous readers. My sincere advice is that the moment you acquire the techniques and knowledge, do not procrastinate.

Neye A. Awonowo, FCA

DEDICATION

This book is dedicated to those who want to make residual income on the internet

ACKNOWLEDGEMENT

http://pandemiclabs.com/blog/wp-content/uploads/2008/02/blogger.jpg&imgrefurl

I express my sincere gratitude to **The ALMIGHTY GOD**, for giving me divine protection and sound health to write this book.

Also, I appreciate the effort of those who made the writing of this book possible. In particular, I appreciate the kind gesture of Mr. Ojo Babasola for making the gathering of information for this book possible.

I equally offer appreciation to Mr. Soji Adekoya, Mrs. Florence B. Dawodu and Mr. Adesiyan Jide for their dedicated efforts to proofread the manuscript (print material). I wish you success in all your endeavours.

My profound appreciation also goes to Mr. Abiodun Awonowo for taking time to review (and to proofread) this book. Thank you for your remarkable effort.

Finally, I also express my gratitude to those who contributed one way or another - morally or financially, to the printing of this book. God will bless you all beyond your expectations.

I thank you all for your support.

Olawale Onasanya © 2011

Please, text or send *free marketing tip, your name, your telephone number, your email address and your comment on what you have gained from this book* to +234(0)805-546-6759 or robest2007@gmail.com for a free marketing tip that will boost your income (revenue).

The probability that we may fail in struggle ought not to deter us from the support of a cause we believe to be just. - Abraham Lincoln

Please, text or send *free marketing tip, your name, your telephone number, your email address and your comment on what you have gained from this book* to +234(0)805-546-6759 or robest2007@gmail.com for a free marketing tip that will boost your income (revenue).

It takes but one positive thought when given a chance to survive and thrive to overpower an entire army of negative thoughts.
– Robert H. Schuller

Please, text or send *free marketing tip, your name, your telephone number, your email address and your comment on what you have gained from this book* to +234(0)805-546-6759 or robest2007@gmail.com for a free marketing tip that will boost your income (revenue).

*"Venture nothing,
and life is less than it should be."*
Malcolm Forbes (1919-1990)

INTRODUCTION

GETTING READY TO CREATING RESIDUAL INCOME:
The Fundamentals

http://freewebs.com/failingz/smiley-face-hug.html

Positive Mindset is the Key to Creating Residual Income

With a positive mindset creating residual income on the internet is absolutely possible. If you think you can get great things done, then getting results will not be impossible. A mind full of positive confessions and aspirations will get positive results as long as such desires are backed up with actions.

A person with a positive mindset does not see problems as insurmountable, but rather as something to overcome with the right mindset and determination to succeed.

To such a person, challenges are stepping stones to his success. Making money online is no difference. You just have to believe in your capability. Believe you will make it if others are making it. With this kind of positive mindset, creating income in several ways on the internet will become a reality.

You may realize after reading through this book (I advise you not to do away with your current job for any online business until you are able to earn more money on the internet than you are currently earning) that you need to do away with your current job (become self-employed) and make a living from an internet business.

Undoubtedly, internet is one of the avenues of making money - for those who have discovered it. Perhaps, you are thinking no good thing can come out of the internet in terms of money making.

Possibly, when you hear about internet business what always comes to your mind is Yahoo! Yahoo! guys (internet scam or fake businesses). Your conclusion is that internet is a platform for dubious businesses (aside good things that you know such as sending and receiving e-mail, online chatting etc).

Well, if that is the way you have been thinking you better have a second thought. The benefits you can derive from the internet are enormous. Aside the fact that it serves as a means of communication via chatting, e-mailing etc., it is also evident that internet is a means of making money.

Internet is certainly a platform that creates and enhances income – you keep making-money in years to come if you know what to do and you do exactly that. You don't have to be awake before making money online – you can earn money while you are asleep. Tell me any offline business that makes money/revenue (buyer gets a downloadable product and the seller earns money instantly) at 1.00am while many people are fast asleep!

Tell me an offline small business that gets its products or services to the worldwide market. Tell me an offline business that incurs little mailing expenses to reach hundreds or thousands of customers and prospects alike. I want you to tell me any offline business that generates revenue in different parts of the world except the multi-national companies that have offices (branches) in many countries.

If you have not discovered any small-scale offline business that could compete with those online, then you need to take your offline business to the internet; where you can make huge profits and incur little expenses – where many opportunities abound. So, the essence of this book is to show you various ways of making money on the internet.

Setting Online Business Goals

It is crucial that you set goals for your online business, as it is to offline. With manageable goals of what you intend to achieve in your mind, you get to know what you are to focus on – and what you are not to focus on, at any given time horizon.

However, don't set goals just for the sake of setting, but rather set achievable goals. These are goals you have the capability to achieve. If you set realistic goals the possibility of achieving same is high.

Don't be afraid to give your best to what seemingly are small jobs. Every time you conquer one it makes you that much stronger. If you do the little jobs well, the big ones will tend to take care of themselves. - Dale Carnegie

---

Mind you, your goals are expected to cover the three time spans, which are short-term, medium-term and the long-term goals. A short-term goal might be to send "thank you message" to a new customer.

You may set-up two more affiliate websites (as a means of boosting your earnings) as your medium-term goal; while your long-term goal will cover a long period of time, say 5 years. You may have a long term financial project in your mind as your long-term goal. Where you want your online business to be in five or six years time may also be your focus – that is your long-term goal. With these goals in your mind, even before you set out, the chances of attaining them are high with proper planning.

It is essential that you put a figure on your goals by putting dates, and times, and also information about what you want to accomplish with them. The idea of quantifying your goals will help you measure your business performance on the internet (compare standards with the actual results).

It is equally good to prioritize your goals. From the outset, you get to know the aspect of your goals you need to deal with first – you consider this the most essential task to execute. When you are through with this, you tackle the next important task, and keep moving downwards until you get to the last. As you do this, you will not be overwhelmed by the magnitude of your goals

It is important that you set realistic short term goals that you can easily build on to medium term span, and thereafter to long term span.

Steps to Online Business Success

Source: http://visual.merriam-webster.com

Your success in online business will not come by chance. It is something you have to work for. As it takes valuable time and efforts to succeed in life, the same time and efforts are needed to succeed online. You cannot achieve success if you do not know what to do in the first place. So you have to figure out what you intend to achieve before going online.

You start off with crucial goals you look forward to achieve on the internet – maybe to earn $100,000, to set up two sites annually etc. Of course, you ought to know what you want to achieve. This is going to be your business map. Remember your goals must be achievable.

Also, let these goals be yours, personal goals – not goals that somebody mapped out for you. So, they are things you have to work out by yourself - never permit anyone to set them for you.

Your goals must be dependent on your capability, skills and of course your needs, so it is not enough just to set them. Thus you have to figure out what your needs are, and the skills you possess to achieving these goals. It is pertinent to know that your success in online business is anchored on these attributes.

Additionally, you ought to determine when your goals will be best achieved. This is a crucial issue that calls for serious consideration. Take for instance, an employee who is willing to profit from internet business should know the best time to give for the online business since he does not have all the time for himself.

However, a self-employed person can carry out his online business activities anytime of the day he considers the best for him; though it is better done at the most productive time of the day. These are the things you have to factor into your goals so as not to set goals that are beyond your reach.

Time Management: A Crucial Skill to Possess

In order to run an effective, efficient and a productive business on the internet – even offline, you need to prudently manage your time. The importance of time management cannot be over-emphasized because your success is centred upon it. This is an invaluable skill every businessman must possess. Without it, achieving success in business, and indeed in life, will be an illusion.

You cannot be productive in business (or get the finest results as expected) if this skill is lacking in your life – if your time is not judiciously spent on things that are important to your business. Thus, learning to manage your time will help you know what you are to put off and what you are not to put off in order to be productive.

> *Waste your money and you're only out of money, but waste your time and you've lost a part of your life. - Michael Leboeuf*

Procrastination does a lot of damages to business. It makes it difficult for you to achieve much in business as you postpone what you ought to do today till tomorrow.

You set business goals with the aim of getting optimal results. To get your anticipated results you need to be focused; and you can't be focused – channel your effort in the right direction, if you always give in to procrastination. That is, if you're not managing your valued time well. When your time is not prudently spent, you will not be able to reach your goals as scheduled.

Therefore, you need to re-adjust your time when you find out that you are not really productive as a result of not being focused. Putting some questions to yourself will help you a lot to discover why you are falling behind your schedule. If you are not able to reach where you envisage at any given time, ask yourself why? By probing yourself, you will discover why you are not where you ought to be; and this will help you to readjust your time and move on.

Putting up an Office in a Place Where There is No Distraction

Source:
http://www.hoopgirl.com/blog/office.gif&imgrefurl

It's not the situation but whether we react (negative) or respond (positive) to the situation that's important.
- Zig Ziglar

Since your business will be running online – possibly at home (home business), setting up an office in a place where there is no distraction (or worse still negligible distractions) will be the best for you. Putting up an office close to the happenings at home will lead to distraction and make you lose focus.

If you are not putting into your business the best (efforts) you ought to put, you will not be productive in business. Hence, your business success will be mired as you focus on unproductive things.

Take the following into account when setting up your home office:

1. Do everything possible to minimize distraction in your home business
2. Let your office be sited in a place that is not close to your household's activities
3. To be productive you have to set up your office for business matters only
4. Ensure you adhere strictly to your achievable work schedule
5. Have a business plan, and make sure you always compare your actual business performance with it (your business plan)

6. Any discrepancy between your business plan and the actual business performance must be addressed without delay.

Statement of Personal Mission

You want to know, in the first place, why you are setting up an online business. Obviously, making a success of an online business is more than knowing the reason for going online – the business you intend to do on the internet, you have to factor in a lot of things in order to achieve your aim of setting up an online business.

Aside knowing the reason for setting up an internet-based business (to make money, to solve a problem etc.); you need to figure out the products/services you want to sell/offer, and the people and/or companies that are going to buy them. In a nutshell, you have to figure out your niche market. That means you are not trying to sell to every Tom, Dick and Harry. You need to answer these questions and any other (questions or ideas) that pop into your mind while brainstorming.

To succeed on the internet selling ebooks, digital photos or whatever, you need a statement of personal mission. With this statement the likelihood of achieving your goal of owning and managing a successful online business is high. If you don't know where you are going how will you know when you get there. Thus, a statement of personal mission is a must for you.

The fore-knowledge of your prospective customers' needs will help you to come up with products/services that appeal to their minds. Moreover, what you intend to achieve on the internet (example, setting up a successful online business) will help you decide the best career path to take – either full time or part time. If you want to make a huge amount of money on the internet you have to consider a full time career path. So, you decide yourself the career path you want to follow. That is your personal decision!

So, a statement of personal mission is something you ought to have as you hope to profit from an internet business.

Conclusion

Remember, to succeed on the internet you need a right mindset – a positive mindset of course. You can make it if you think you can – even if you know nothing about the internet at present.

It is not your aptitude, but your attitude, that determines your altitude. - Zig Ziglar

Furthermore, set realistic goals and adhere strictly to them, and equally learn how to manage your time and never postpone whatever you can accomplish now.

Finally, as you read through this money making guide, you will discover many avenues of making money online – of course, creating residual income. Obviously, you would make money, even enjoy financial breakthrough, on the internet if you put into use the money-making techniques, written in this book, you have the capability to do.

Join me in chapter 1 to learn how to package and sell information products for a living.

CHAPTER 1

ONLINE INCOME #1

INFORMATION PRODUCTS:
Earn Residual Income From Info Products

http://www.amazon.com/

Introduction

A sure way of generating residual income online is by creating information products for sale. Internet is saturated with information that is just the reason why a great number of people access it on a daily basis to getting information that meets their needs.

Internet is not only an avenue of accessing valuable information across the globe, but also a pedestal where business transactions worth billions of dollars, if not trillion(s), are carried out annually.

In view of this, making money on the internet through information products is one of the wisest business decisions anyone could take. It is therefore not out of point, if you build business around it (selling information products). Certainly, selling information products is one of the lucrative online investments.

> *To think creatively, we must be able to look afresh at what we normally take for granted.*
> *- George Kneller*

Actually, information products are products that possess informational attributes – that is, they have informative outlook, and they come in different forms such as ebook, newsletter (e-zine), training video and audio, digital report, software, teleclasses, live seminar, online course etc.

#1 Make Money Selling Ebook

Preamble

Ebook is an essential material that is used not only to disseminate information, ideas, techniques etc., but also to solve people's problems (through unique information/ideas emanating from it). Therefore the significance of ebook cannot be over-emphasized.

A growing number of internet users today have undoubtedly increased the production and distribution of ebooks online. This also buttresses the point raised in the foregoing paragraph.

Aside the fact that ebook is a source of making money; it is also a means of driving traffic to a website through viral marketing. Over the years, people have used ebooks to drive huge traffic to their websites by giving them away to their subscribers or selling them at reasonable prices with Private Label Rights (PLR).

In spite of all these, print book is still valuable today. Of course, print materials are invaluable materials and their positive influences cannot be overlooked. Imagine, if there were no print materials in the society (or the world at large), lives (of men) would have deteriorated – more marriages would have collapsed, poverty rate would have escalated beyond measure, the rate of illiteracy would have increased tremendously – just to mention a few.

The Uniqueness and the Attributes of EBooks

However, ebooks are unique materials because they possess some special attributes which cannot be seen in any print books. For instance, ebooks require little production cost and no handling cost. You don't have to spend huge amounts of money on printing before offering them for sale.

Aside the above, ebook could be purchased on the internet the moment payment is made (via any online payment tool), and it (ebook) requires no inventory cost – you need no garage or warehouse to store your ebook.

In addition, the beauty of an ebook is that it possesses interactive attributes. You could add surveys (for people to fill) and hotlinks (hyperlinks) to your ebook to enable reader visit any of the hyperlinks without typing the

URLs on the browser every time. Order form could also be added for buyer to fill in etc.

Submission of manuscript is likewise removed unlike print book. You don't need to submit any manuscript before you offer your ebook for sale on the internet. All you need to do is write and upload your ebook to your website – if you have one. In addition to that, you ensure that the right tools are in place to ease the sale of your ebook. The tools include autoresponder, payment processing tools, sales copy etc.

Another unique attribute of an ebook is that it could be delivered on the internet without your involvement or that of your representative(s); and whether you are asleep or not, your ebook could be sold (it does not need your intervention).

You don't need a huge amount of money to print ebook unlike print books which calls for a huge amount of money (several hundred dollars or several thousand dollars) depending on the number of copies you intend to produce. The publisher might tell you the minimum number of print book he would produce at any given time. You really do not need to print ten (10), fifty (50), hundred (100) or more copies of your ebook before you offer it for sale. In fact, you need not to even print a copy. All you need to do is write and place the same on the internet for sale via a website (or a blog).

Having known the uniqueness and attributes of an ebook, it is worthwhile if you can write one and place it on the internet for sale. That will take us to the next subtopic – Reasons for writing an ebook.

Reasons for Writing Ebook

The question you need to ask yourself (at this very moment) as you are reading this book is "why do I have to write an ebook"? It is important that you know why you are writing an ebook so as to know what to write about.

In actual fact, something ought to have moved (prompted) you to go into writing. Of course, you want to make money - that is an obvious reason. Aside that, there are still more reasons for writing an ebook.

Perhaps, you have seen a vacuum to fill or a problem (or problems) to solve. Maybe you have seen some critical needs you intend to meet. These are some of the reasons why people write ebooks – even print books.

Undoubtedly, there are lots of reasons for writing ebooks. It may be to solve a problem in a unique way. Before the advent of Microsoft Windows software computers were not user friendly then when compared with the present time. The man, Bill Gate, saw the need to improve the way computers were being used those days, so came up with a product - Microsoft Windows Operating System. Since its inception, Microsoft (Bill Gate's Company) has produced many versions of this software such as Windows 95, 98, XP etc., for the use of computers at various times. He came up with a solution so as to improve the use of computers, having seen the problem.

We will always have one problem or another to solve while we are still living on this planet (earth). People who think big always think beyond problems that are confronting them. To such people coming up with solutions will not be a herculean task. They may even have many ways of solving a peculiar problem because they think outside the box.

Unfortunately, there are people who do not think straight. The kinds of things they say often show they are pessimists – they often think in negative ways. I don't think I can do this, I don't think I can succeed in this line of business; I don't have the competence to execute the task … and the rest. If you fall into this category, it is high time you thought straight and do away with all these stuff … - I can't …, I don't...

Don't find fault. Find a remedy. - Henry Ford

If you think you cannot achieve great things in life, you will never get great things done. You will never succeed on the internet – even in this mortal world, if you think you cannot. The achievers are those who believe in their capabilities. You need to believe in your potential – your extraordinary abilities or qualities God has deposited in you (that is your God's given talents). You need to discover and exploit these potential (if you have not).

If you think you cannot write an ebook, you will never come up with one written by yourself. You can only be successful when you think and act positively. So, be a positive thinker!

Ebooks help to give instructions and disseminate information to people looking for solution to their problems – ways of getting problems solved. A person that lurk in a chat room (on the internet) looking for information on money making will be enlightened by an ebook that talks about money making.

If you have ideas people could benefit from you can turn the same to an ebook and make a living from it (ebook). Publishing ebook is not as difficult as print book. All the stringent conditions often associated with a print book are removed. You need no publisher before making your ebook available for sale. You don't need to submit any manuscript as well.

Ebook can also serve as a means of promoting a website – your own website. You can write a five page ebook and give it away in order to promote your site (or the product you are selling).

Writing ebook will not only earn you money but also make you an expert in your chosen career. You then become an authority in your profession – someone that people will seek advice from. You may even have the potential to author many books that deal with many areas of human needs.

Writing ebook could bring a considerable financial reward to you. This is a venture that will earn you money in years to come. You are sure of making residual income online as you commit your time to writing series of ebooks that deal with people's problems. When your ebook solves a problem (or some problems) some people are encountering, they may visit your site any time another problem comes up (unmet needs) – to see whether you have authored another ebook that deals with that too, having regarded you as an expert (of course, an authority in your field of study).

You can even recruit affiliate marketers to help you promote and sell your ebook in turn for sales commission of probably 20% or more. That is a share of your sales revenue!

However, you need to look for saleable keywords - keywords that yield high investment returns. You will do well selling information product on the internet that cover a specific niche (not a generic product – a product for every person). You can research the internet for a saleable niche and invaluable ideas for your information product.

A lot of profitable keywords could be found online. More importantly, keywords that solve people's essential problems are always profitable. For instance, ebooks that show people how to make money on the internet, how to lose weight, how to drive traffic to a website, how to ..., etc will sell - these are some of the niche products that sell online. It is better to focus on a profitable niche than making an effort to reach every Tom, Dick and Harry.

Indispensable Guidelines to Writing an Ebook

Having explained the reasons for writing an ebook, you still need to know what it takes to write one. Knowing the benefits of an ebook is not enough, but writing one yourself (or getting one written for you) is what matters most. That is how to earn residual income online.

The above subtopic (indispensable guidelines to writing an ebook) is essential to your ebook writing success, especially if you have never written any ebook. If you don't know what it takes to write an ebook – even a print book, you might be wasting your valuable time for being ignorance of these facts (guidelines). A company that embarks on a project without schedule is likely to spend more time and resources than expected.

With a persistent mind you can achieve much in your endeavours. A mind that is ready to go extra mile for success will not shudder. It will never take no for an answer.

Whatever you vividly imagine, ardently desire, sincerely believe, and enthusiastically act upon... must inevitably come to pass! - Paul J. Meyer

When we are determined to get something done and we are committed to it, success will definitely come. Our dreams and aspirations will become a reality.

Hence, knowing the benefits of an ebook would not translate into cash except you convert the ideas (knowledge) you've got (and still going to get as you keep reading) in this book into an ebook, and invariably into cash. Knowledge that is not applied will not yield a fortune on the internet.

Writing bit by bit (little by little) is a sure way of achieving your book writing project. You may have to write a chapter (or a few pages) on a daily or weekly basis. All through the period of the project you ensure that you keep track of the happenings, otherwise you won't be able to complete your project as scheduled. However, you may need to re-adjust your time when you are not keeping up the pace.

Surely, it may take you weeks or months (or probably few days) to achieve this (to finish your writing), but the fact is that with concentration you will get the work done.

The bottom line is that you are now the author of an ebook. What a great achievement!

You start by identifying your niche market – the market you want to serve. That means you have to figure out your audience and invariably their needs, and ensure that these needs are offered to them. It is as simple as that!

Brainstorming and exploring the internet (or print materials on any subject that interests you) are two sure ways of getting an attractive topic for your ebook. As soon as you are able to generate three or four ideas, you have to brainstorm so as to narrow down these ideas (ideas you've got) to one. Hence, the most profitable idea among those generated above ought to be the title of your ebook.

Having known what to write about, then you need to brainstorm on the topic you've got (a lot of ideas could be generated while you are brainstorming). In addition to this, you ought to explore the internet (including offline materials) for more relevant ideas for your ebook.

http://gallantpotts.files.wordpress.com/2010/06/148_th inking_person2.gif&imgrefurl

You can ask yourself some questions such as the ones below:
How relevant is your ebook?
How will it influence your readers positively?
Who are your readers?
What problems are they having?

Your answers to the questions above, coupled with the ideas that popped into your mind (make sure you put them down) are part of the concepts (information) that will form the content of your ebook.

You have to decide how you want your ebook to be sold, either through your website or a third party site – site that sells ebooks.

Setting a project deadline is an important issue you should not overlook. Never start a book project (or any project for that matter) without a deadline – the time you want to finish the writing of your ebook. It is a great mistake for anyone to embark on a project without envisaging when the project will be completed. So, you have to set a deadline at the outset in order to remain focus. There is a tendency for you to finish your ebook ahead of schedule when you are focused. Hence, setting a deadline is crucial to your success.

The foregoing paragraph could work for any project, aside book project (ebook or print book). In fact, whatever project you want to embark upon, ensure that you have a time schedule. It helps you to be focused and invariably get your desired results.

By the time you read through this book in your hand, you will have every reason to believe that you can make it on the internet through one or more money-making techniques mentioned therein. However, before you launch into any of them, ensure that you have a schedule of what you intend to achieve - this will enable you get your anticipated results. Of course, a working time schedule (a time schedule that works) is what you need.

A project that supposes to take ten (10) days to complete, if you assign five (5) days to same you would not get the work done. And if you do, the possibility of over-working yourself is there so as to meet the deadline. So, setting a strenuous time schedule will not be right for you, most especially for your health. You need not to over-work yourself before getting things done. However, it does not mean you cannot readjust your schedule. Surely, your schedule could be re-adjusted if situation calls for that.

You also need to fight against procrastination in your life – a serious fight indeed. You cannot succeed in any endeavour (including internet business) if you always give in to procrastination. Procrastination will not make a realistic time schedule work for you. So, never postpone till tomorrow what you can accomplish today. Procrastination hinders progress and causes poverty as well.

Don't start living tomorrow, tomorrow never arrives. Start working on your dreams and ambitions today.
- Unknown Author

Getting Ideas for Your Ebook

There are places – offline and online - where you could get ideas for your ebook. Obviously, you can get useful information from print materials such as books, journals, newspapers etc. Internet is another beautiful place where ideas could be gotten. I still believe internet is the best place to get invaluable information for your ebook.

Through interviews you can also get ideas for your ebook. You interview someone or people with expert knowledge of the topic you want to write about. With that, you are going to get some ideas to start off your book project.

A lot of avenues of generating ideas are right there on the internet. You can get tons of unique information in search engines such as Google, Yahoo!, Bing etc. You can as well visit some discussion forum sites for invaluable ideas that are related to the title of an ebook you intend to write.

You can even visit www.amazon.com, a site that sells books on the internet. Indeed, internet is a great place to get invaluable ideas (information) for your ebook. Free ebooks are available on the internet in large numbers. All you need to do is explore the internet for these numerous ideas.

In addition, as you cultivate the habit of writing - articles and more ebooks – your writing skills would improve. So, give yourself to writing. Make sure you always write about something such as memo, letter, article etc. Also, as you commit your time to reading books, there is every possibility that your writing skills would improve to some extent.

Lastly, if you are not good at writing (or you don't have flair for writing) the best thing to do is to engage the services of a freelance writer. You may be charged per hour rate or a fee. It is better you engage a ghost writer to help you write your ebook than being left out of the possibility of making money on the internet through information product. This is a site where a ghost writer could be hired www.elance.com

Another way of packaging an ebook is to team up with someone who has flair for writing. Let him turn his writing skills (his written communication skills) to an ebook as you supply the expert knowledge. If you are good at writing, but lack knowledge of what to write about team up with someone that has what you do not have – the expert knowledge. With that, you both become co-authors and share the profit.

Make Your EBook Attractive to Your Readers

You must ensure that your ebook possesses some attributes to make it unique and attractive to your reader. You can add short stories, quotations, graphics, pictures etc to grab your reader to keep reading.

You can make your points clear to your reader by using bullets and numbers – this will make your ebook user friendly.

Also, endeavour to use fonts of moderate sizes so as not to strain the eyes of your readers. Both your spellings and your grammar must be thoroughly checked. In addition, index and bibliography could be added to make your ebook user friendly.

How to Compile Your Ebook When You Are Through with Your Writing

- When you are through with your writing, the next thing is to get an ebook compiler – software that converts your writing into Portable Document Format from Microsoft Word.

- In order to make your ebook user friendly, make sure you use a compiler that makes use of hyperlinks, graphics, order form, surveys and security feature (to prevent unauthorized access to your ebook). This will help you protect the content of your ebook.

You can visit the sites below for your ebook compiler:

http://www.pdf995.com
http://www.mindlikewater.com/ebook_software_publisher.html

- You also need graphic design software for your ebook cover. A good graphic cover art will make your ebook attractive, and invariably enhance sales. So, you need to use high quality graphic design software.

Here is the site for ebook cover art www.killercover.com

http://www.trafficsources2.com/UserFiles/Image/ebook _cover_front.jpg&imgrefurl

Setting the Price

After you have written and compiled your ebook, you have to determine the price it will be sold. You must ensure that your price is not too low. The price should be based on a perceived value – the value your prospects think the ebook worth.

Set a price you think your prospective customers can afford. You may need to conduct market research on this in order to envisage the price your prospects can afford.

In addition, you have to consider the worth of your ideas, not your production costs now. If you think your ideas worth thirty dollars ($30) then you set your price at thirty, regardless of your production costs. It might cost you a negligible amount of money to produce an ebook, and sell the same at an exorbitant price because your pricing decision is based on the value of the ideas you are exposing to people, and not the cost of production.

In the case of a print book, the cost of production must be factored in so as to determine the selling price, but an ebook could be sold at a price over the cost of production.

At times, your goal may determine the price you are going to charge for your ebook. If your purpose of writing and selling an ebook is to promote your site or to make a name for yourself, not minding what you get from it in terms of financial gain, you may charge a low price for your ebook.

You could also charge low if you plan to keep customers for a long term. You set a low price to attract people to buy your product now and in the future.

Set a high price if your ebook is full of invaluable information people are willing to acquire. For instance, if it is produced to solve problems you can set a high price.

Your pricing decision could also be based on the time span of your ebook project. Aside that, your efforts, and of course, the skills you put into it are other factors that will determine the price of your ebook. You have to pay off yourself for all the efforts you put into writing the ebook.

Getting Your Ebook Out and Profiting from It

Getting a good number of payment processing tools is another crucial issue you have to consider. You want to know which of the payment options you should opt for – the ones that will not make you lose prospective customers and, of course, money such as Paypal, 1shopping cart and Clickbank, MasterCard, VisaCard. If your country is not listed on paypal website or any of the payment processing tools mentioned above (which you intend to use), do a search on the internet for any sites or web hosting sites that render this service [setting up an online account].

Another way to sell your product (if your web hosting company could not help) is to make your bank account number – local bank account, available to your prospects on your website. All you need to do is send the product to your customer (the person that put money into your bank account) via his/her contact information – email address, residential address or postal address – the moment payment is made and confirmed through a message (text or email) from your bank.

You will also need a website (or a blog) to sell your info product, except you want to take an alternative route to get your ebook sold – sell through an affiliate marketing programme (via another person's website).

If you choose to sell your ebook through a website, then you have to create one (if you don't have a site). Aside the above, you need to get autoresponder software to build a mailing list.

Without traffic you cannot sell anything through your site. Traffic is an essential issue you need to take very serious if you hope to make money online through an ebook. Endeavour to read chapters 14 and 15 later on so as to know how to drive traffic (visitors) to your site.

Though affiliate marketing is one of the means of selling digital products such as ebook, software etc. on the internet, you still have to sign up with an affiliate marketing site that sells affiliate products. All you need to do is upload your ebook to the site after signing up. With the army of recruited affiliates working with such a site you would be able to sell your ebook.

With what you have read so far (knowing what it takes to produce an ebook and the price to charge for same), you still have to consider the marketing strategies to employ to bring in the profit – the reward for your labour. After all, the purpose of writing an ebook in the first place is to make money.

You will need a sales copy to promote your ebook. If you can not write a sales copy yourself, you may have to get (hire) someone to write it for you. You also need a press release to enable you launch your product (ebook).

Sales copy is really crucial to selling your info product on the internet. It states the benefits (ensure these benefits are highlighted) your prospective customers are going to get for buying your ebook. The essence of the copy is to get your prospects bought your ebook.

In addition, the opening sentence of your sales copy should be persuasive. It should be written in such a way that will appeal to your prospective customers' minds. You can use this to grab your readers to read through your sales copy. Some may buy your ebook as a result of this.

The cover art of your ebook should be designed in a special way to sell your ebook. An attractive cover art will attract your prospective customers to buy your product. This ought to be the reason for putting it there in the first place. Of what use is a cover art that does not add value to a product.

Another way of getting people to buy your ebook is to extract the content of your ebook for an article you are going to use to promote it. Please make sure this article is published on website(s) that accept(s) articles for publication (in order to drive traffic to your site). The excerpts could also be used for a short report that you can give away so as to drive traffic to your site.

You can also add to your sales copy a hyperlink to your free ebook (that is the web page link of your free downloadable ebook). Endeavour to offer valuable free ebook (you can get free ebook from any of the sites that promote free stuff) while making an attempt to sell your own ebook. However, ensure that your download link seems effortless to ease access to your ebook.

Finally, your "thank you page" should appear immediately a sale is made. You use the page to thank your new customer for buying your product.

Aside that, the page (thank you page) should also be used to convey an essential information regarding your product – how to use your info product, or any other vital information such as email address, telephone number(s) etc. You can as well use the page to sell your back-end products – other related products.

#2 Setting-up an E-zine Business

Preamble

E-zine sites are websites that advertise (promote) their products and services to their prospective customers and customers alike through newsletters - periodical electronic magazines (e-zines).

E-zine sites also sell advertising space through periodic newsletters they normally send to subscribers on regular intervals – daily, weekly or perhaps monthly.

Setting up an e-zine business will make people regard you as an expert in your chosen career. As you build a mailing list of subscribers who are interested in your e-zine (newsletter), you will have the opportunity to sell your products or services to them via periodic newsletter.

You can also generate money from advertising space because some of your subscribers will be willing to place ads on your website or your newsletter - especially if your e-zine site has a huge subscriber base, say thousands of people.

For instance, an e-zine site with 20,000 or more subscribers can generate a huge amount of revenue from advertisements, affiliate marketing programmes and even sell its own services or products.

In addition, you can build a mailing list with an e-zine business (without any of your subscribers visiting your site) from any site you are promoting via periodic newsletter you often send to your subscribers.

You can learn how to set up your own e-zine (newsletter) business via this website: www.ezineuniversity.com

Getting Information for Periodic Newsletters

Getting information (ideas) for your e-zine business is crucial to your success because without it you can not keep in contact with your mailing list via periodic newsletter.

Your e-zine site could be listed in e-zine directories on the internet. You could as well get articles for your newsletter from one of these directories you are linking with. These are articles sent by websites' owners to e-zine sites listed in the directories, and the purpose (of sending articles to e-zine directories) is to generate some traffic to their sites (that is webmasters' sites).

Anyone who wants to use any of these articles must not alter the resource box placed at the bottom of the published article to enable the writer gets some traffic to his/her site.

The resource box should entail writer's website (URL address), business slogan and an email address. With resource box, the writer will be able to drive traffic to his site.

Here are sites to visit for free articles:

www.ezinearticles.com
www.web-source.net
www.ezineseek.com/resources/article/index.shtml

How to Get People to Sign Up for Your Newsletter

- Put your subscription form in all the web pages of your site, and ensure that each page is linked to the home page.
- Though your newsletter is free, you still have to tell your visitors the benefits they will get for signing up for it. Also, you need to tell them the type of information your newsletter will convey and the period they will be getting it.

- Put a pop-up window on your site entry page – a small window that opens up any time the page is visited. The small window comes up with an offer to subscribe to your e-zine.
- Offer free report (free ebook) so as to attract people to sign up for your newsletter. You can also give your prospective customers free ads to make them sign up for your newsletter. Free blog could as well be offered to your visitors to achieve the same.
- Another way of getting subscribers is by listing your e-zine in free e-zine directories. This is a great way of promoting your site. Visit the sites below for listing:

www.zinebook.com
www.ezinesearch.com
www.ezineseek.com
www.newsletteraccess.com

- You can also drive traffic to your site by publishing articles on e-zine directory sites. With this, you are sure of getting people to visit your site as they click on your website URL which is placed at the bottom of your articles.
- Another way to get traffic is to buy traffic that relates to your niche market if you can afford it. If you are buying subscriber list you have to figure out how much each subscriber will cost you. For instance, if you are buying a subscriber list of 5,000 people for $200 – that means you are paying $ 0.04 per subscriber.

  Here are sites that sell subscriber lists:
  www.newslettersforfree.com
  www.bestnewsletters.com

- You can drive traffic to your site by posting your announcement on announcement list at www.emailuniverse.com

Finally, make sure you send welcome message to your newsletter's subscribers. The message will entail what they are going to get from your e-zine, and how to opt-out if they want.

#3 Other Information Products You could Sell

1. Selling training videos and audios online
2. Teleclasses – consulting services via telephone
3. Selling digital products (ebooks, software etc) - other people's products (affiliate marketing)
4. Organize online courses – computer training, online forex training etc.
5. Live seminar programme
6. Selling special report online

This is a wonderful story of Jeff Walker who started his online business without any internet marketing experience. Please, make the time to read this wonderful story.

Jeff is an Internet marketing guru and consultant who first appeared in the mid 1990s. His most popular item is the Product Launch Formula, a step by step product launch marketing strategy program relevant to any product or niche. As well as selling his Formula, Walker makes instructional videos and teaches workshops on product launch topics. His focus is helping small companies start with small, profitable product launches to get their business of the ground. While Walker mostly works with small companies, he has also helped get the careers of fellow internet marketing gurus off the ground by helping them plan product launches for their marketing products. In fact, helping out other marketers is how Walker first found the spotlight. Helping John Reese launch his Traffic Secrets internet marketing course made Walker popular among marketing veterans and beginners alike.

Currently located in Colorado, Walker started his online business in 1996. At the time, he had no experience with internet marketing. He uses his story of starting his own online company with zero initial investment as an example for beginning marketers. Walker also publicizes product launches and success stories from other online businessmen who started their companies with little to no upfront financial or time investment. Walker has been blogging on his Powered Internet Marketing blog since October 2005, several months after the first release of the original Product Launch Formula. Product Launch Formula 3 was released in June 2010.

Unlike other online marketing consultants who focus on Pay Per Click or specific advertising strategies, Walker teaches entrepreneurs the basics of planning a product launch. One of the biggest marketing ploys used by a wide range of internet businesses, product launches is a concentrated advertising drive to publicize a new product and attract customers. Walker is often credited as being the internet marketing guru who made the product launch as a marketing strategy as popular as it is today.

Walker's Product Launch Formula, now in its third edition, takes beginning marketers through the steps of planning and implementing a successful product launch. The Formula has received rave reviews from users who cite it as being easy to use, comprehensive and effective. Past users note that the Product Launch Formula will not help a beginner find a product to sell; instead, it helps users sell whatever product they have found. The program is one of the best available if the marketed product has already been decided on and acquired. In Product Launch Formula, Walker not only gives users a detailed timeframe layout for their product launch, he also writes exactly what should be said in each email and how each aspect of the launch should be conveyed. Walker also offers some consultation benefits with the purchase of his Product Launch Formula.

Walker has recently launched another product to help online marketers and Product Launch Manager. This program takes product launch implementation to the next step and helps users keep multiple, simultaneous launches organized. This program also advocates running other companies' launches as another money making venture and gives instructions on keeping that more complex system organized. Walker's other products include the Product Launch Blueprint and its upgrade, and the Product Launch Formula Coaching Program.

One of the winning aspects of Walker's products is his ability to build relationships with existing and prospective users. Through his blog, website and Twitter account, Walker reaches out to his audience, draws them in and keeps them interested. The marketing techniques he uses to sell his own products are the same as what is in his Product Launch Formula program. Walker uses surveys and pre-launch research to determine the course of his marketing, regardless of whether he is planning a short term launch or a more drawn out campaign.

Source: AffiliateLifestyle.com

In the next chapter, I will not only show you how to discover good affiliate marketing programmes but also reveal to you how to profit from same using a mailing list.

Go confidently in the direction of your dreams! Live the life you've imagined.
- Henry David Thoreau

CHAPTER 2

ONLINE INCOME #2

AFFILIATE MARKETING:
Make Money By Selling Other People's Products

http://www.tokunbo.com.ng/listings/Studio.cfm?/#theLink

Introduction

Affiliate marketing is a marketing programme that enables you (an affiliate) earn commission whenever a prospective customer/client buys a product from your affiliate merchant's site through your efforts. Affiliate marketing is one of the popular means of making money on the internet.

Some companies have seen the need to extend their businesses online in order to boost their profits. Indeed, one of the marketing strategies they employ to get their products/services sold is affiliate marketing. You can use the same marketing strategy to reach a lot of people online if you have a product or service to sell.

The sales commission may be between the range of few percentage to seventy five (75%) of the product's price (unit sale). When a sale is made through an affiliate, he gets paid for his effort – so he gets a share of the pie.

However, your affiliate commission is based on the products you are promoting. Durable products such as computers, electronic gadgets, etc. tend to command low affiliate commissions compared with the digital product such as an ebook.

The merchant company makes available the product, sales copy, tracking tools, website to sell the products, payment processing system, customer service, a link to its site, and also handles sales orders. Thus the affiliate is then left alone to promote the products he has chosen. So, most of the work is done by the merchant (the product's owner).

Upside of Affiliate Marketing for the Affiliates

- An affiliate can generate income in multiple ways by selling many affiliate products and back-end products
- You make more money, as an affiliate, when you promote two or more products from the same merchant
- The hassles of getting marketing tools to work with are removed – you need not to write a sales copy, handle/ship any product, and order for any product. All these are taken care of

- To top it up, you get a free marketing training – training that costs you nothing (money) to acquire. What a plus!

Here are sites that show how affiliates are ranked in terms of payments:
http://www.refer-it.com
http://www.associateprograms.com
http://www.clickquick.com

Through affiliate marketing you can generate residual income by creating a mailing list. This will enable you to sell back-end products to your customers, aside the initial sales.

Let's use the hypothetical example below to illustrate how to profit from affiliate marketing programme.

Let us assume that you joined an affiliate marketing programme that paid 60% commission on every ebook sold. Let's assume that each ebook was sold for $40, your commission then would be $24 (60% of $40). That is a good commission!

So, in order to get the product sold, you bought a cheap e-zine advertising space for $10 a month. You also subscribed to a free autoresponder (from www.getresponse.com).

See the results beneath:

1. **Affiliate Marketing Programme:**
- Selling Price= $40
- Sales Commission (60% of $40) = $24

Marketing tools:
- E-zine Advertisement = $10.00 for one (1) month
- Autoresponder software = $0 (from getresponse.com)

- Targeted at businessmen who wanted to boost sales revenue by 50%
- E-zine advertisement to reach 1,500 subscribers (on one e-zine site)

Investment cost = $10.00:
- Investment cost was equivalent to the cost of placing an e-zine advertisement

Prospective customers:
- People were led to affiliate link through sales copy
- Prospects' email addresses and names were collected through autoresponder
- Sent newsletters to follow up your prospects for one month

Results:
- 20 subscribers (people who joined the mailing list)
- 4 copies of ebook were sold

Affiliate net sales commission:

	$
Sales commission ($24 multiplied by 4 units)	96
Expense (E-zine advertisement)	(10)
Net sales commission	$86

Plough-back your net sales commission

Assuming that the sales commission generated above is to be ploughed-back into same affiliate marketing programme (placing ads in three e-zine sites with high membership lists at this time).

2. Affiliate Marketing Programme:
- Same as above (same affiliate marketing programme)

Marketing tools:

- Placed three (3) e-zine ads at $17 per advert for another one (1) month
- E-zine advertisements with subscriber lists of over 18,000 (over 6,000 average)
- Autoresponder software = $0 (from getresponse.com)
- Targeted at businessmen who wanted to boost their sales revenue by 50%

Investment cost (plough-back part of the sales Commission):

- No investment cost because the previous profit was re-invested in three e-zine advertisements.

Prospective customers:

- People were led to affiliate link through sales copy
- Prospects' email addresses and names were collected through autoresponder
- Sent newsletters to follow up your prospects for a month

Results

- 100 subscribers (people who joined the mailing list)
- 20 copies of ebook sold

Net sales commission:

	$
Sales commission ($24 multiplied by 20 ebooks)	480
Balance {previous net sales commission minus ploughed-back sales commission ($86 – 51)}	35
Net sales commission (current net sales)	$515

Note: At the end, the net income of $515 was realized from 24 copies of ebook sold (4+20) – generated a mailing list of 120 subscribers in turn (20+100). This resulted into $4.29 per lead ($515 divided by 120 leads). That would be $4.29 sale commission for every subscriber that joined the mailing list.

With the example above, you can see how profitable affiliate marketing programme is. The net sales commission will escalate as sales revenue increases. So, the possibility of enhancing sales revenue is evident with increased advertising campaigns.

However, you should not depend only on sales commission; make effort to build your own mailing list via autoresponder because of the attendant benefits.

> ## *It is the nature of thought to find its way into action.*
> ## *- Christian Nevell Bovee*

With a mailing list you can generate more money in the future from back-end products.

Upside of Building a Subscriber List (A Mailing List)

The aim of generating subscriber list is to enhance your revenue in the future. That means whenever you have another product that is similar to the one(s) you have already sold, you quickly refer your subscribers to this product. This is the beauty of generating a mailing list. You can equally exchange your mailing list with someone's list that has a product (to sell) similar to the one you sold previously.

You can also sell the list if you like, to those who need it to enhance their sales revenue. Can you imagine selling your mailing list to four or five people after you have used same to generate a lot of money? What a great gain, indeed!

These are websites that can help you to set up your own affiliate programme: www.cj.com

Discovering Good Affiliate Marketing Programme

- A solid affiliate merchant must have quality products to sell.
- Affiliate marketing programme with a two-tier commission is also a good one. You get paid as an affiliate and earn more money anytime someone joins the affiliate marketing programme through you.
- The affiliate marketing programme is free. You don't have to pay any dime before you become an affiliate.
- You have the necessary tools to work with – sales letter (newsletter), affiliate link, tracking tools, website to sell the product (or related products), and you need not to handle sales orders, payment processing systems, and customer service.
- You are offered a good commission, say 20% - 75%, on digital products. Sales commissions on hard products are usually low.
- An affiliate merchant that pays life-long sales commission is a good affiliate marketing programme. You get paid when someone buys a product through you at first, and keep earning commission as long as the person keeps buying the merchant's products – that is referred to as long-life commission.
- Does the company sell high quality products and enjoy as well good patronage in terms of increased sales revenue?
- Does the company have strong tracking tools – to track sales, impression and hit, that its affiliate marketers can logon to check online (if they desire)?
- Does the company have a strong financial report? A company without a strong financial report will not be able to stand the test of time – economic or financial crises.

- An affiliate merchant that sees the need to expand its customer base by coming up with new quality products, and products update. This will create more customers, and invariably lead to the recruitment of more affiliate marketers in order to reach the new customers. The bottom line is that more sales commission will accrue to the affiliates – that is a good affiliate marketing programme.
- Affiliate marketing programme that pays for impression and hit is also a good one.
- If the affiliate link leads a prospect straight to the product page, not the home page, more sales commission will be earned by the affiliate marketer. Also, this is a good affiliate marketing programme.

Criteria for Choosing the Right Niche for Your Website/Affiliate Marketing Programme

You pick a niche that you have passion for – something that you like very much. Something you are able to do very easily and very well (be naturally good at doing). It might be what you always think about or the experience you garnered in your place of work.

You think of a problem you have the capability to solve. A problem you love to solve without taking much time to think about it. This may be the best niche for you. Because your mind is in it you are likely to succeed without much effort.

Aside that, whatever niche you intend to choose let it be a profitable one. A niche that turns in high profit on your online business – that is what you need.

Join an affiliate merchant that has a good reputation – don't join affiliate marketing programme just for the sake of money, please.

Choosing the Best/Profitable Niche for Your Affiliate Marketing Programme

When you take a time to cogitate, some salient ideas will pop into your mind – please make a concerted effort to jot them down so as not to forget.

The next thing to do is to choose the best three or four ideas/concepts from those that popped into your head.

To determine the best niche (possible and profitable concept) amongst those you have just narrowed down (to 3 or 4) you research on the internet to find the best concept that has a huge/high demand (searches) and a low supply. The point is this; you are looking for a concept (keyword) that has a high demand – in terms of people that search for the keyword, and a low supply (low supply here means the number of websites that exist for this keyword using Google search engine).

If the demand for this keyword is higher than its supply, then the keyword is said to be profitable. Thus, a keyword that has the potential for making money amongst the shortlisted ideas/concepts is regarded the best niche for your affiliate marketing programme.

Downside of Affiliate Marketing Programme

One of the pitfalls of affiliate programme is to focus on many affiliate marketing programmes at the same time. If you are promoting many products at the same time, the tendency for you not to devote your time to these affiliate programmes is there. You may not achieve much if you are not focused. It is, therefore, better you focus on one or two affiliate marketing programmes at the same time rather than running many affiliate programmes.

Secondly, concentrating on instant sales (trying to get people to buy your product instantly – not pre-selling) is another pitfall of affiliate marketing programme. If you do not pre-sell your prospective customers you would not achieve much. To pre-sell means to warm up your subscribers. You focus on giving them valuable content until they fall in love with your content – by keep visiting your site for valuable content, and subsequently you sell your product to them.

Thirdly, if you fail to gather the names and the email addresses of your prospective customers, then you would be making a great mistake. How will you get them to buy your back-end products when you do not build a mailing list? So, while you are selling your affiliate product(s) consider the benefit of building a mailing list.

Another pitfall of affiliate marketing is to create a web page for all the products you are promoting. Really, you ought to create a web page for a product (or similar products).

When the content on the web page is not different from the one on the sales page your web page ranking will fall due to repetition. The moment your website drops its ranking on major search engines - Google, Yahoo! Search etc., you start to experience less traffic, and this will invariably reduce your sales commission as an affiliate.

Another pitfall of affiliate marketing programme is that when an affiliate does not have the right tools to work with. A solid affiliate merchant will make the right tools available because they want their affiliates to succeed – of course, this will bring success to them (affiliate merchant) too. If the right tools are not made available sales revenue and sales commission will decline.

Lastly, another mistake any affiliate marketer can make is not to believe in his/her capability. As an affiliate, if you think you will not succeed, you won't. You will only succeed when you manifest a positive attitude. With a positive mindset, you will not be overwhelmed by any challenges that come your way. Success is guaranteed when you think and act in a positive manner. As a man thinks so he is. If you think you will succeed, you will succeed, of course. However, if you think the other way round, you are going to get the other results. Indeed, your success or failure in business is the product of your thoughts and your actions.

Nurture your mind with great thoughts, for you will never go any higher than you think.
- Benjamin Disraeli

Tips for Affiliate Marketing Success

Get your site updated regularly with fresh content, and ensure that you measure the statistics you are getting from your advertising campaigns. With that, you get to know the advert(s) that is/are lucrative and the one(s) that is/are not.

Endeavour to list your affiliate marketing links in the directories of affiliate marketing programmes. This will help you drive traffic to your affiliate site(s).

Also, your newsletter must be updated on a regular basis, so that your subscribers will have every reason to keep reading your newsletter and probably buy your product(s).

In addition, endeavour to pay serious attention to any questions your prospects and clients/customers may ask you. Whenever you receive emails from your customers and the prospects alike, take a time to respond to them. Make sure you respond promptly to these emails.

Whatever sample of a product or advert you intend to give away to your prospects make sure you sort out the same.

As you keep up with your affiliate marketing programme you may realize that you need to equip yourself with some vital information. Do not hesitate to do so. Take advantage of any opportunity that comes your way to improve your learning.

When a prospect becomes a customer, make sure his/her name is moved from the prospect list to a customer list.

You may have not more than 3 affiliate marketing programmes at any given time. The first affiliate marketing programme may be used to build a mailing list. The second for creating residual income – income that accrues to your affiliate account through sales commission {you keep earning affiliate income as long as the people you referred to your merchant's site keep buying your affiliate merchant's product(s)}.

Here are sites that show the list of residual income affiliate marketing programmes:
www.lifetimecommission.com and www.cj.com

Then, use the third affiliate marketing programme to earn more money from your customer list (subscriber list) by selling back-end products to them.

Check out the directory of affiliate marketing programme at http://www.associateprograms.com

Check this site out for software that helps you create your newsletter – http://www.instantnicheemails.com

Whenever a prospect buys your product, make sure a 'thank you message' is sent out to that person (you can send a free report to him later).

Keep sending newsletter (emails) to your mailing list in order to keep the relationship. You can send free report, and special promotion of a product or service oftentimes. And whenever you have a back-end product to sell, you tell them about it. Do not stop offering them free stuff (but you have to be careful the way you do it – not too much).

Take a couple of minutes to read the underneath success story of Allan Gardyne – an affiliate marketing expert ...

Who is Allan Gardyne?

Have you heard of that apparently mythical guy who lives by the beach and makes a living from affiliate programs? That's me. The story is true.

I'm a former journalist. I live with my wife, Joanna, at Rainbow Bay, in sub-tropical Queensland, Australia.

If you read articles saying we live at Tuan, a tiny fishing village so small it doesn't have a shop ... well, that used to be true.

Then we bought an apartment overlooking Golden Beach, and more recently one at Rainbow Bay.

(We usually spend summers in New Zealand and winters in Queensland, Australia.)

What does Allan Gardyne do?

Joanna and I run AssociatePrograms.com, a comprehensive directory of affiliate or associate programs. It was launched in January, 1998.

I set up a hobby/business on the Internet in 1996 because I wanted to be my own boss. Since then I've made a lot of mistakes and gone up a few dead-end alleys – failing forward, as the optimists say – and eventually quit my day job in 1998.

We've turned a hobby into a thriving business which now has three full-time employees and a fluctuating number of part-time employees.

I don't just write about affiliate programs. I work at this stuff. Nearly all of our revenue comes from affiliate commissions.

You don't have to make the mistakes I did. Life's too short for that.

To learn how you can make a good living with affiliate programs, subscribe to the Associate Programs Newsletter. It's crammed with insider tips and reviews of affiliate programs.

I give tips from the winners – people who are earning good money TODAY – from affiliate programs.

What else does Allan Gardyne do?

He founded PayPerClickSearchEngines.com, the first directory of pay-per-click search engines. If you're looking for highly targeted, cost-effective advertising occasionally as cheap as one cent per click, that's the site to go to for information.

Another of my sites is LifetimeCommissions.com, the first directory of affiliate programs that pay lifetime commissions or residual commissions. I like being first to do something.

Keyword orkshop.com, run by my business partner Jay Stockwell, is another one. It's the most comprehensive site on the Internet for reviews of keyword research tools, which are essential for anyone who has a business on the Internet.

I teamed up with Jay in 2005 and Jay set up an office Burleigh Heads, Queensland, Australia. Our first major project was SpeedPPC.com, a system which enables you to do PPC marketing incredibly faster and more efficiently. Check out the enthusiastic testimonials.

We also own a number of other affiliate-driven sites on a variety of topics. They derive their income from affiliate commissions and Google AdSense.

It's a nice way of living. You can live and work from wherever you like, being your own boss.

Allan Gardyne

AssociatePrograms.com

1101/255 Boundary Street

Rainbow Bay

Coolangatta

Queensland

Australia 4225.

Visit AssociatePrograms.com now.

Allan Gardyne

I don't advertise this AllanGardyne.com web site. It was created just for curious people like you.

I will show you how to make money via Google's advertising programme – Google Adsense, in the next chapter.

CHAPTER 3

ONLINE INCOME #3

GOOGLE ADSENSE:
How To Make Money With Google Adsense

Real Estate in Dubaiwww.TheFirstGroup.com
Amazing Capital Growth on Luxury Apartments $400,000. Great Returns!
Ads by Google

Google ⁿ [   ] Search

⊙ Web ⊙ PublishingCentral.com

http://www.google.com/asdense/home

Introduction

Google Adsense programme had been around for quite a while. It actually came into being less than a decade ago. Adsense is a programme Google uses to reward websites' owners who help to publicise its Adwords programme.

Google often shares its advertising revenue (revenue coming from Google Adwords) with people who signed-up for adsense account (people that have AdSense java coded ads on their sites); and they (these people) get paid when those ads (placed on their sites) are clicked.

> *Stop the habit of wishful*
> *thinking and start the*
> *habit of thoughtful wishes.*
> *- Mary Martin*

Why Google Adsense?

Making money through Google adsense is one of the best stakes for you, and you start by filling in Google Adsense application form placed on the internet. This book will guide you how to sign-up for adsense account and also make money from the same (coupled with the essential information that you ought to know which appears in the subsequent paragraphs and subtopics).

Setting up an adsense account is not difficult once you are ready to follow the laid down rules and regulations (Google's policies). Adherence to these rules is what makes it easy to sign up (so, there are no hard and fast rules here). Surely, you will get to know these essential rules – Google policies, as you keep reading.

Perhaps, you are thinking what is Google adsense all about? What does Google adsense entail? Through Google adsense you could earn a huge amount of money if you are able to drive huge traffic to your site. The moment any of the ads (Google ads) placed on your site is clicked you (the owner of the site) get paid.

As earlier said, Google adsense is a programme that Google uses to reward people who help to publicise its adwords programme. The amount of money Google pays these people – webmasters, e-zine publishers etc., ranges from little cents to a few dollars based on the ads (Google) placed on their sites (placing of ads on any site is usually based on the site's concept).

Nevertheless, any Google adsense site with low paying ads could still earn a reasonable income if such a site could generate huge traffic, and attract substantial clicks as well.

Naturally, the content on your web page will determine the ads Google will serve you.

Additionally, make sure you add new content (update your content) to your site on a regular basis. This is a sure way of attracting traffic (a huge number of people for that matter), and new ads to your site.

Any webmaster or e-zine publisher could make a reasonable amount of money through Google adsense if he/she builds a website around a high paying keyword - keyword that yields high payout per click, and also drive traffic (a huge number of visitors) to his/her website.

Building (or creating) many websites (or weblogs) with different keywords is another way of making more money through adsense. With one adsense account, you can set up many adsense websites (even 10 sites).

It is, however, pertinent to know that you will not get paid if your site gets no click; and if there is no traffic (visitor) your site will not get any click (and you are not permitted to click on any of the ads placed on your website – so as not to get banned by Google). In fact, no man can succeed online without traffic (except those that render services via third party sites – who really do not have their own websites). So, you have to employ some traffic generating techniques to bring visitors to your adsense website(s), if you really want to make money through this programme.

Of course, there are many ways to drive traffic to your site – please endeavour to read chapters 14 and 15 of this book later (to see various ways of getting people to your site).

A site that is filled with problem-solving content (example, money making, weight loss etc) will likely attract traffic, and generate income from Google adsense programme.

A lot of people are looking for ways to solve their intimidating problems such as unemployment, poverty etc. Hence, it makes sense if you can come up with a site's concept that will solve any of these problems. Of course, this is a sure way of profiting from Google adsense.

When your visitors know you have something of great value to offer they will come visiting. They will not come occasionally but frequently. Tell me, when you came across a site that offers invaluable stuff didn't you visit same over and over again? I guess (not really sure) you did! If you keep visiting a website because of invaluable materials (free information) such as ebook, investment tips, quality content etc you are getting there, in that case you should expect some (or better still many) of your visitors to do the same.

Really, you have to figure out your niche market. Aside this, you need to find out the problems this market is having and how to solve it (through a product/service).

You may ask yourself some questions which may help you come up with a product for your niche market:
Why do people surf the Net?
What do they surf for?

Keywords like how to ..., overcoming debts, making money ... always appeal to people's minds. So, creating a site concept around any of these keywords will be a good decision. More importantly, since traffic plays a pivotal role in making money on the internet every effort must be geared to drive traffic (visitors) to your site.

As you fill your site with quality content on a regular basis (coupled with some in-bound links coming from quality sites), the chance of your site being ranked high in notable search engines after sometime is evident.

Money never starts an idea; it is the idea that starts the money.
- W. J. Cameron

Getting Prepared for Adsense Account

Getting approval from Google is crucial to making money through adsense programme. It is obvious, you will not make any dime if your site is not approved by Google. To put it briefly, you will not be able to profit from adsense programme if Google's approval terms are not adhered to (if the terms are not obeyed). Google will ensure that your site meets its approval terms, which are adsense terms of service, before accepting it.

Firstly, make sure you read over the Google's Adsense Terms of Service to know whether you are qualified for Google adsense or not. That is how to get started. This, of course, is one of the things you ought to consider before setting up a website (or a blog) for Google adsense programme.

Visit Google Adsense for details:
http://www.google.com/adsense

Note that Google does not approve a website that is still under construction. It must be complete. Thus, if you want your Google Adsense account to be approved you must present a complete website.

If you present an incomplete site (site that has no content is regarded as incomplete) Google will definitely reject it. That means your site will be turned down rather than being accepted for Google adsense programme. Website with reasonable information (not pornographic pictures) is one of the Google's adsense terms, and you have to adhere strictly to it.

Aside a complete site, you need to study adsense quality guidelines in order to have an intimate knowledge of the things you ought to have on your website (and things you ought not to have). For instance, Google does not accept a pornographic site. So, a thorough study of the quality guidelines will do you good. You can have a print out of this via www.google.com/webmasters/guidelines.html.

Please, endeavour to read through the program policies as well. These three materials – TOS, Program Policies, and Quality guidelines are essential for your adsense approval. Since getting adsense approval is mainly dependent on these materials, it is worthwhile to take a time to read them. So make sure you read these materials before applying for Adsense. The above materials, and a complete application form (coupled with a complete site) are the things you need to know in order to take part in Google adsense programme.

Mind you, the fact that your website is approved does not mean you cannot get banned by Google in the future if you fail to adhere strictly to its laid down rules.

You are expected to abide by Google's terms of service (TOS) even after approval. Google will not tolerate any website that contravenes its laid down guidelines before or after approval.

You need to brainstorm and equally do a search on the internet (via notable search engines) for some specific keywords in order to know the keywords that are profitable for your website(s) before signing-up for adsense.

Also, you have to decide either to go for a blog or a website for your adsense programme. Whichever you choose, you still have to decide the company that will host it for you (website/blog). Additionally, you have to figure out the features you want to see in your web hosting package if you choose to set up a website. For a free blog, you can use www.blogger.com.
You can also use www.wordpress.com for a free blog hosting (wordpress.com is good as blogger.com)

How to Open Google Adsense Account

First of all, you fill in the adsense account application form which is available at www.google.com/adsense/g-app-single-1. See a copy beneath:

Welcome to Adsense   What is AdSense? | Already have an account?
Please complete the application form below.

Website Information

Website URL:

w w w .yourdomainname.com

⁇

• Please list your primary URL only.

• Example: www.example.com

Website language:

| English — English | ▼ |

• Tell us your website's primary language to help our review process.

☑   I will not place ads on sites that include incentives to click ads.

☑   I will not place ads on sites that include pornographic content.

Contact Information

Account type: ⑦

| Individual | ▼ |

Country or territory:

| Nigeria | ▼ |

[!] **Important** - Your payment will be sent to the address below. Please complete all fields that apply to your address, such as a full name, full street name and house or apartment number, and accurate country, ZIP code, and city. Example.

Payee name (full name):

• Your Payee name needs to match the name on

your bank account.

• Payee must be at least 18 years of age to

participate in AdSense.

Contact name (full name):

Street Address:

City/Town:

State:

ZIP: [?]

• To change your country or territory, please change your selection at the top of this form.

☑ I agree that I can receive checks made out to the payee name I have listed above.

Telephone Numbers

Phone: 2348055466759

Email preference:

We'll send you service announcements that

relate to your agreement agreement with Google.

☑ In addition, send me periodic newsletters

with tips and best practices and occasional surveys to help Google improve AdSense.

How did you find out about Google AdSense?

Other

Policies

AdSense applicants must agree to adhere to AdSense program policies (details)

☑ I agree that I will not click on the Google ads I'm serving through AdSense.

☑ I will not place ads on sites involved in the distribution of copyrighted materials.

☑ I certify that I have read the AdSense Program Policies.

☑ I do not already have an approved AdSense account (Click here if you do.)

Submit Information

The first information you will see in adsense form is **Website's URL,** and you need to fill in this information (**under Website Information**). Website URL is the domain name you intend to use for your Google adsense programme (www.online-business-success-tips.blogspot.com is an example of a domain name). You are expected to use only one URL account for your Google adsense programme even if you wish to own more than one websites.

After your URL, your **Website language** is the next information you are expected to supply (still under **Website Information**). This is the language your site will be published. Of course, you are expected to choose ENGLISH (if your site will be published in English) from a drop down menu as your website language.

Under website language, there are two important statements in bold type which you are expected to check (that is to tick by clicking on them one after the other). These statements are stated below (still part of **Website Information**):

1. *I will not place ads on sites that include incentive to check on ads*
2. *I will not place ads on sites that include pornographic content*

The next information on adsense form is the type of account (***Account type)***. Select BUSINESS if you are employer and you have twenty (20) or more people working for you. If not, choose INDIVIDUAL.

Aside the Account Type, you also need to supply the underneath information (still under **Contact information category**):

Country of territory – your country of birth or nationality (eg. Nigeria, USA)

Payee name (full name) – your full name including your surname (this is the name that will appear on your cheque)

Street address – your residential address (this will be used to send cheque to you, except you choose to receive cheque through postal agency – post office box)

City/Town – where you reside at present

Postal code – as you click on the question mark (**?**) beside the postal code, you will be directed immediately to the NIGERIA POSTAL SERVICES' WEBSITE where your postal code will be accessed. Click on your STATE from a drop down menu, and then your local government (FEDERAL GOVERNMENT RECOGNISED LOCAL GOVERNMENTS only) to get your postal code. Please keep this information for future reference. If you reside in ISOLO, under OSHODI /ISOLO LOCAL

GOVERNMENT in LAGOS STATE, your postal code will definitely be **100003** (at the time of writing). There is another important information on this website (Nigeria Postal Services) which are not useful for adsense programme, but might be useful to you in the future **such as International Airport Complex and arrival Hall**. **Please note that immediately you select NIGERIA as your country of territory, *zip code* which appears on the form as you logon will change to *postal code*.**

State – the state where you reside

When you are through with the information above, it is time to check (click on) the important statement below:

I agree that I can receive check made out to the payee name I have listed.

Telephone number - make sure your telephone number includes international code, country code and your local code if you are not using GSM number (if you are using GSM number, do not include the first zero (0) after typing your international and country codes – see this example 009-234-805-546-6759. While 009 represents an international code, 234 is the country code (for Nigeria). Please make sure your telephone number(s) is/are typed correctly.

Email preference – Endeavour to read the statement below as you fill in Google adsense form – **we'll send you service announcement that relate to your engagement with Google.** You may also check the statement below if you wish but not compulsory – **in addition, send me periodic newsletter with tips and best practices and occasional surveys to help Google improve adsense.**

How did you find out about Google adsense? **–** select the right option from a drop down menu

Policies **– Adsense applicants must agree to adhere to Adsense program policies (details).** Please endeavour to read through Google's Adsense policies.

In addition, make sure you check the three statements below (underneath Google Adsense policies):

1. I agree that I will not check on the Google ads I'm serving through ad
2. I certify that I have read the adsense program policies (please make sure you read Adsense program policies)
3. I do not already have an approved adsense account (click here if you do)

The next thing you need to do is submit your adsense form by clicking on **submit information**.

Finally, after clicking on submit information, you have to wait for a moment for your Google adsense form to be processed.

Mind you, it may take three business days for your site or blog (the URL address you provided in your adsense form) to be inspected by Google's member of staff. Google will surely contact you via your email address after your site has been inspected.

Techniques for Making Money with Adsense...

Source: Google Adsense Secrets Revealed... All About Residual Income with Adsense - pages 10 to 13 of 44

What works on one website may not work well on another.

However, according to Google and many successful AdSense

publishers, placing a rectangular ad unit just below your headline, but above the main content of your page, will yield higher clicks. Also, placing link ads in, above, or below your navigational links will also increase clicks.

There is more to it than targeting keywords. The content must be accurate. It must be readable and understandable by visitors.

You should use all of the search engine optimization techniques as possible when building your site. Not only will this attract the right ads, but it will also help your site to move up in the search results, for the purpose of driving traffic to your site.

You want your site to look nice, to be informative, and to load fast. You want it to attract the right ads. You do not want anything on your pages that will irritate your visitor, such as blinking, blinding text or music.

Make it a site that you would want to visit, and then ask an uninterested party, such as your neighbour (not your best friend or your mother) if it is a site that they would want to visit, if they are interested in the topic.

Now, you are ready to place the Adsense javascript code on your pages. Log in to your Adsense account. Click on the Adsense Set up tab at the top of the page.

First, click on Channels, and set up a Channel for the topic of your site. This will come in handy later on, when you are analyzing which of your sites is pulling in the most money.

Next, click on palettes, and create a color palette that matches your site well. You want your Google ads to blend into your site.

If they stand out like a sore thumb, they will get fewer clicks, simply because people really do try to avoid advertisements.

Above – the perfect example of a well optimized ad placement

Source: Instant-Adsense-Templates.com

You can use the ad units (boxed in) on other sections of your site. Those who have been in the Google Adsense game for a while have done years worth of testing on the topic of ad unit placement.

You want the ads to look like content on your site. Once you've set up a palette that matches your site, click on products. Choose Adsense for content to create your ad units.

Here, you can choose ads that are enclosed in a box, or ads that are more free standing, but still just text links. It is a good idea to choose the link unit to add above or below your navigational links, and you can design your site navigation links to look just like the Google link units.

Ideally, you will use 'text ads only' as your setting. Note that Google has limits as to how many Google ads can be used on your page, please check with the TOS (Terms of Service).

As you can see, it is fairly easy enough setting things up, but it takes a lot more thought and effort than that. What you must remember is that you often only make a few cents when someone clicks an advert. Each click can pay as little as one cent, but I have seen amounts up to three dollars. The example below

The most successful Adsense publishers are targeting keywords that pay the most amount of money. These Adsense publishers use a variety of tools to find out what the high paying keywords are. These tools include keyword research tools, such as Word Tracker and Keyword Elite.

http://www.wordtracker.com

http://www.keywordelite.com

They spend a great deal of time researching those keywords, finding out what the top keywords are, in terms of number of people searching for them, and what word combinations are being used. These are words and phrases that they will target in the content of their sites.

Next, they determine which of those top keywords topics pay the most money per click. Those who have been in the Adsense "game" for a while are not going to build sites that target keywords that only pay one cent per click!

These Adsense publishers use the tools that Google provides to help determine which keywords are paying the most to the publishers. Unfortunately, you won't find these tools inside your Google Adsense account.

No, you need a Google Adwords account for this - http://adwords.google.com/

You see, Google has two programs that work together: Google Adsense and Google Adwords. Business owners use Google Adwords to promote their products and websites and it's those ads that are shown on your Google Adsense ads.

The business owner pays Google for each click generated on your website, and Google pays you for the service.

It's free to create a Google Adwords account. Once created, you just get in there and start using the tools that are there to see how much bids are for the keywords that you've discovered using keyword selection tools such as Word Tracker and Keyword Elite.

By doing this, you have access to the same information that the people who are paying for ads have, and this helps you to build more profitable Adsense websites.

This is a nice trick that Google won't tell you about, and that most Adsense publishers won't care to share with you. Having a Google Adwords account is the key to finding out which keywords are going to pay you the most amount of money per click.

Choosing the right high paying keywords, however, isn't everything; you need traffic – and lots of it, simply because low traffic sites will NOT make you a full-time living. This is why most publishers have more than one websites.

They find the top keywords in terms of number of searches, figure out the keywords from that list that pay the most amount of money per click, and then build sites, lots of sites...

A successful Adsense publisher may have sites on topics such as fishing, weight loss, video games, making money, and many more. When you have multiple sites, you can make a nice living with a mid level amount of traffic to each site.

If you have hundreds of sites, like I have, you can make a living even with low traffic. So, here is some food for thought: The more traffic you have per site, the fewer sites you will need to earn a living from Adsense.

Finding Profitable keywords

Based on one or both of the following:

Word or phrase (one per line)

Weight Loss

Website   Only show ideas closely related to my search terms

Keyword	Competition	Global Monthly Searches	Local Monthly Searches	Estimated Avg. CPC
weight loss	0.51	7,480,000	5,000,000	$3.07
weight loss tips	0.67	201,000	110,000	$2.82
weight loss plan	0.61	165,000	90,500	$4.71
weight loss pills	0.83	246,000	165,000	$2.36
fast weight loss	0.75	201,000	135,000	$2.53
quick weight loss	0.77	201,000	135,000	$2.26
weight loss programs	0.86	135,000	110,000	$3.28
weight loss help	0.52	40,500	27,100	$3.91
weight loss foods	0.46	60,500	40,500	$2.44
rapid weight loss	0.63	90,500	49,500	$2.59
weight loss calculator	0.43	74,000	49,500	$1.48
weight loss recipes	0.48	60,500	40,500	$1.74

easy weight loss	0.74	40,500	27,100	$2.13
la weight loss	0.57	74,000	60,500	$3.18
healthy weight loss	0.57	110,000	74,000	$4.00
diets for quick weight loss	0.85	135,000	74,000	$1.69
safe weight loss	0.75	33,100	22,200	$2.70
fast weight loss tips	0.7	18,100	9,900	$1.26
quick weight loss tips	0.68	12,100	6,600	$1.69
weight loss success stories	0.33	27,100	14,800	$1.75
weight loss secrets	0.5	14,800	9,900	$2.42
weight loss diet	0.61	450,000	246,000	$2.42
weight loss motivation	0.35	14,800	8,100	$1.96
effective weight loss	0.74	33,100	22,200	$2.12
fastest weight	0.78	14,800	9,900	$2.33

loss

fast weight loss diet	0.79	33,100	18,100	$0.00
weight loss products	0.81	49,500	27,100	$2.49
green tea weight loss	0.59	74,000	40,500	$2.46
weight loss supplements	0.78	90,500	60,500	$3.92
weight loss forum	0.23	22,200	9,900	$2.81
medical weight loss	0.68	74,000	60,500	$2.67
weight loss for women	0.6	90,500	60,500	$2.81
weight loss solutions	0.66	14,800	9,900	$7.24
weight loss exercises	0.38	40,500	18,100	$1.79
best weight loss	0.64	246,000	165,000	$2.37
weight loss clinic	0.6	74,000	49,500	$2.80

weight loss chart	0.59	33,100	12,100	$1.11
weight loss system	0.69	27,100	18,100	$9.11
natural weight loss	0.74	74,000	49,500	$2.51
weight loss blog	0.2	22,200	14,800	$1.80
hcg weight loss	0.88	74,000	60,500	$0.05
best weight loss program	0.85	14,800	9,900	$3.39
best weight loss pills	0.91	33,100	27,100	$2.56
walking for weight loss	0.27	27,100	14,800	$1.49
weight loss workouts	0.36	18,100	14,800	$1.69
online weight loss	0.71	49,500	33,100	$2.65
weight loss hypnosis	0.82	74,000	49,500	$3.32
weight loss drugs	0.49	27,100	14,800	$2.00

weight loss spa	0.85	14,800	9,900	$4.40
best foods for weight loss	0.22	12,100	8,100	$1.59

Go to page: 1   Show rows: 50 ▼

Table 3.1
www.adwords.google.com/select/KeywordToolExternal

How to Interpret the Searched Results

Building adsense website around **weight loss** is more (highly) profitable venture than **weight loss tips** due to huge Global Monthly Searches of 7,480,000 coupled with an estimated average cost per click (estimated average CPC) of $3.07 in comparison with 201,000 searches and $2.82 estimated average CPC as shown above. By virtue of the information above, one can build Google adsense around weight loss.

Make sure you carry out your own keyword (or phrase) search before you build your Adsense website. This is a sure way of creating a profitable adsense site.

How to Search For a Keyword (or Phrase) on Google.Com

To search for a keyword (or phrase) on the internet via google.com, as shown in the results above, you type this   URL www.adwords.google.com/select/keywordtoolexternal on the web browser.

Subsequently, you type in your keyword (or phrase) below FIND KEYWORD (as indicated in Table 3.1 above), and click on search.

At the end of the search, the engine would reveal the results of the searched keyword (or phrase) including the related keywords. See the above searched results on weight loss for details (please ensure that the bold type statement **ONLY SHOW IDEAS CLOSELY RELATED TO MY SEARCH TERMS** is not checked/ ticked). In order to see the estimated average cost per click (for all the keywords shown above) ensure that you click on download (download your searched results to your computer via MS Excel) **on the left side near the following sub-headings: keyword, competition, global monthly searches, local monthly searches and local search trends.**

Google AdWords

Traffic Estimator

Summary (per day)
Average Estimated CPC
$1.93 - $2.71
Total Estimated Clicks
2,223 - 2,788
Total Estimated Cost
$4,286.93 - $7,550.07

Get traffic estimates
Word or phrase (one per line)

Weight Loss

Max CPC$ $200.00

Daily budget$ $10.00

	Keyword	Global Monthly Searches	Local Monthly Searches	Estimated Avg. CPC	Estimated Ad Position	Estimated Daily Clicks	Estimated Daily Cost
☐	weight loss	7,480,000	5,000,000	$2.32	1.31	2,505	$5,918.50

| 1 | Show rows: | 50 ▼ |

1 - 1 of 1

Important Note: We cannot guarantee that these keywords will improve your campaign performance. We reserve the right to disapprove any keywords you add. You are responsible for the keywords you select and for ensuring that your use of keywords does not violate any applicable laws.

© 2010 Google | <u>AdWords Home</u> (Table 3.2)
<u>www.adwords.google.com/select/KeywordToolExternal</u>

How to Get Traffic Estimates

You first of all go to <u>www.adwords.google.com/select/KeywordTo olExternal</u>, and click on traffic estimates. Subsequently, you type in your keyword (or phrase) – using weight loss as an example, maximum cost per click, say $200.00, and your daily budget (let's say $10 as indicated above) on the traffic estimates webpage on the site. The estimated average cost per click at the time of reporting was $2.32 (as shown in the traffic estimates results on weight loss above). That is the average cost per click for an adwords campaign.

I have presented below the amazing success story of Google. This article focuses more on straight points rather than lengthy explanations.

Let us see some quick facts & figures:
Google was named after the number "Googol" which means one followed by a hundred zeros. It is the top search engine with over fifty percent market share. It is one of the top three most visited websites. Over four thousand million searches are conducted every month on it.

It has localized websites for over 150 countries. There are over 117 language options to view your Google page in. This search engine is supported by a backend of over 80,000 to 100,000 servers.

The Story Of Google, Inc:

The founders of Google are Larry Page and Sergey Brin. It started in 1996-97 in Stanford University when both of them were students there. They received startup venture capital of $100,000 in 1998 from Andy Bechtolsheim. In 1999, they received $25 Million in venture capital. This further bolstered their growth. The growth in terms of employees, search queries & revenues was always increasing. The primary focus has always been on search.

Some Major Milestones of Google

Over 100 Million searches were being conducted daily by 2000. They started their advertigrams AdWords and AdSense in 2002-03. They went public in 2004 with an initial public offering in USA and raised $1.67 Billion. They formed major partnerships with NASA & AOL in 2005. The Google stock was added to S&P 500 index in 2006. The company employment crossed 10,000 employees in 2007.

The author writes extensively on a variety of topics and works in the social media arena. The author writes text messages and advises and consults for social networking content for myspace graphics and myspace surveys.

Article Source: http://ezinearticles.com/?expert=CD_Mohatta

You will learn in chapter 4 how to boost your revenue by taking your services to the internet.

Vision without action is merely a dream. Action without vision just passes the time. Vision with action can change the world.
- Joel A. Barker

CHAPTER 4

ONLINE INCOME #4

MAKE MONEY SELLING YOUR SERVICES:
Take Your Services To The Next Level

http://www.subaquatica.com/images/pandarosa_noctur
nal_pandas_mural.jpg&imgrefurl

Introduction

Do you know you can make residual income online? Yes, you can! You can make a handsome amount of money on the internet by making your services available to people who need them around the globe.

Truly, Internet has made it possible for people to take their services to different parts of the world (small-scale, medium scale and large-scale businesses can extend their services to the outside world which was not common before the advent of internet). It would be unreasonable, therefore, to restrict your services to your local market when you could get more patronage by offering your services to the global market through the internet, and invariably enhance your earnings.

Indeed, pharmacists, mathematicians, auto mechanics, caterers, fitness trainers, landscapers, sales agents, dentists etc can take advantage of the internet to enhance their earnings. In actual facts, internet is virtually for all businesses (everyone) – be it accounting firm, investment consulting services, pharmaceutical store, travel and reservation business etc.

A pharmacist could boost his earnings by rendering medical consulting services for fees to people who need such. An accountant could render accounting services online. He can equally bid for business plan on www.elance.com and www.gofreelance.com.

Even if you cannot operate computer, not to talk of browsing the internet, you can make money on the internet if you are prepared to acquire computer knowledge (internet training). In actual fact, if you are serious about making money online, getting internet training would not be a problem. You may engage someone who has knowledge of computer and internet to teach you how to browse the internet or better still enroll on an internet training programme at any of the schools (computer schools) in your vicinity.

Some people dream of success...
while others wake up and work
hard at it. - Author unknown

So, what are you waiting for? Are you not going to get your own share of the pie? If the second statement (question 2) is of interest to you, then keep reading.

How to Exploit the Internet to Get Your Share of the Pie

As a matter of fact, a lot of opportunities are there on the internet. For instance, internet helps people to market their services to the outside world. Aside the fact that the possibility of enhancing your revenue generation is high by taking your services to the internet, you can also use the internet to leverage your business – to discover various ways (avenues) of enhancing your revenue with the same services.

So, taking your offline services to the internet is one of the wisest decisions you can take. However, you have to do the right things (get the right tools to work with, and equally drive traffic to your site) if you hope to make money on the internet via your services. If you have a website you have to promote it - that is the sure way of making residual income online.

Even if you don't have a website of your own, you can bid for jobs on freelance sites. Really, you have to devote your time, and of course your attention, to search and bid for jobs on freelance sites if you are serious about making money on the internet.

A dentist can offer dental treatment consulting services online. In fact, I read about a dentist, a resident of the United States, who made a lot of money via his website. Some of his patients/clients even travelled tens of miles away for his services. Aside this, he gets new patients on a monthly basis because he uses his website to build trust and credibility. So, when you pre-sell your clients (not seeking for immediate sales) you are building trust and credibility.

A pharmacist can set up a website to sell advertising space to drug manufacturing companies, companies that sell pharmaceutical apparatus (equipment), educational institutions that offer pharmacy (or/and any related disciplines), etc.

He can equally make money from info products (by selling ebook that relates to his site's content, special report on new medications), teleclasses – special consulting services via telephone, affiliate marketing (selling other companies' products such as drugs, medical apparatus etc on commission), and referral fees (earning referral fees from local pharmaceutical stores, hospitals, etc.). However, he has to consider how to attract traffic (visitors) to his site.

As a pharmacist, he can drive traffic (a reasonable number of people) to his site if he fill it with valuable content, and he pre-sell his visitors. As he keep providing his visitors with fresh and hot content (and sending quality newsletter that relates to his site's niche), they will fall in love with his site, and keep visiting it. For instance, he may fill his site with content such as **diets for quick weight loss**, **weight loss tips, best weight loss pills** etc.

When you pre-sell your subscribers (or visitors) with **free**, **well packaged** and **quality** content (for your site and your periodic newsletter both), you are building trust and credibility in their minds. So, some of your subscribers (visitors) will be willing to buy your services because of the credibility you have built.

Just do what you do best.
- Red Auerbach

Source: www.uschemist.com

Generic Viagra	Cialis Generic	Singulair Generic

 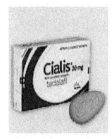 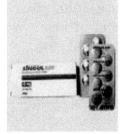

100 mg - 20 Tablets	20 mg - 40 Tablets	10 mg – 90 Tablets
Special Price $40	**Special Price $75**	**Special Price $96**
ADD TO CART	ADD TO CART	ADD TO CART

Actos Generic	Amoxil Generic	Lamisil Generic

 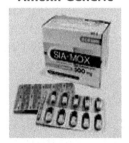 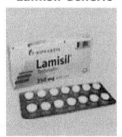

30 mg - 30 Tablets	500 mg - 30 Capsules	250 mg - 28 Tablets
Special Price $40	**Special Price$33.40**	**Special Price $77**
ADD TO CART	ADD TO CART	ADD TO CART

You can check out these sites:

www.drugstore.com
http://pharmaceuticalshop.net/

http://www.valuepharmaceuticals.com
www.uschemist.com

Subsequently, you monetize your site (generating money from your site through referral fees, selling advertising space and info products, rendering medical consulting services, teleclasses, and any other means of generating income as mentioned earlier) after you have pre-sold your visitors (people that visit your website) and those who subscribe to your e-zine (periodic newsletter).

> *The immature mind hops from one thing to another; the mature mind seeks to follow through.*
> *- Harry A. Overstreet*

The beauty of the internet is that you can render some special consulting services via telephone without being physically available to (present with) your clients (though not applicable to all services). In addition, you can even sell other people's products such as drugs, software etc via affiliate marketing programme or set up an online store (for drugs or any products you choose).

As you pre-sell your subscribers, you will not only sky-rocket your site traffic, but also generate more money as a result of increase in conversion rate (a high rate of people taking decisions to buy your products/services).

So, anyone who wants to make residual income on the internet must be prepared to build trust and credibility. As you plan to sell your services online, via your site, trust and credibility are vital issues you must take into account.

Do you know that a barber (a person whose job is to cut men's hair), newspaper editors, surveyors, language translators, copywriters etc could also boost their revenue generation using the wheel of the internet?

For instance, a newspaper editor can write articles (get a weekly or monthly column) for international journals - even use same to build an online business for a living. A language translator can enhance his earnings by helping people translate any language to another language. Of course, internet has a place for other professionals around the world – virtually all professionals. Any business can exploit the internet not only to make its services known to the outside world, but also to make an incredible (a handsome) earnings.

So, whatever expert knowledge you possess you can make money from same. You can profit from your hobbies - anything you can impart to people.

A computer programmer can market his web design and consulting services via any of the freelance websites or better still set up a website to render the same services.

A secondary school English teacher can set up an online English tutorial to educate people on the Use of English. A financial analyst, of course, can set-up a website to educate people on how to invest wisely in equity investment, and in turn generate handsome investment returns through membership subscriptions to special investment reports.

A dry cleaning outfit can use internet to reach its prospects and customers alike via bulk text massages. Customers might be informed of any promotional package the outfit is offering. Through this strategy, some prospects would be converted to life-long customers. This method could equally be employed by a barber – a person whose job is to cut men's hair.

Vision is not enough; it must be combined with venture. It is not enough to stare up the steps; we must step up the stairs. - Vaclav Havel

---

Artists, economists, architects, engineers, legal practitioners, and business administrators can also benefit from the internet.

In fact, these professionals would be able to generate more money by marketing their services online. For instance, an artist can generate more revenue by selling his digital art online via www.payloadz.com. An engineer can bid for projects on www.elance.com.

Indeed, you need to check out this site www.elance.com for various jobs (projects) that are available for freelance professionals. All you need to do is create an account (sign-up) with the site – that is to create a profile, and then start to bid for projects as soon as you are connected with employers via emails. Visit the site for further information on setting up a profile account. The underneath job directory was obtained from www.elance.com.

Web Development Jobs | Programming Jobs | Design Jobs | Multimedia Jobs | Writing Jobs | Translation Jobs | Admin Support Jobs | Sales Jobs | Marketing Jobs | Finance Jobs | Consulting Jobs | Legal Jobs | Engineering Jobs | Manufacturing Jobs |

http://www.thesalon16.co.uk/media/images/large/sal16
-inside2.jpg&imgrefurl

Real estate companies could also enhance their revenue generation via the internet. I even know some websites (local and international online-based outfits) that advertise their real estate on the internet.

In fact, the benefits of the internet cannot be over-emphasized. The benefits are numerous. That is why you need to put internet technology to good use to enhance your revenue generation. If you are not satisfied with your current revenue/earnings, then you need internet - to boost your revenue/earnings.

One of the recognized freelance websites on the internet is www.elance.com. Another one where people could get a lot of online jobs (services) is www.gofreelance.com, but you have to sign up before you can bid for projects.

Your services could also be rendered via www.freelancer.com and www.rentacoder.com. Whichever site(s) you wish to do business with, the essential criterion, aside the fact that you need to register with the site(s), is to bid for jobs (projects) within the ambits of your expertise. Also, make sure you render high quality services to your clients.

Supposing you need a financial consultant to help you write a business plan, all you need to do is post your project (say business plan on equity investment) on any of the freelance websites so that people can bid for it.

In fact, I came into contact with a freelance site (not www.gofreelance.com) when I was surfing the internet early year 2010 (I suppose), where a project on business plan was posted.

The beauty of rendering online services via Gofreelance.com is that projects (jobs) are sent to your email address often, but you have to consider the monthly fee (recurring fee) of $49.95 if you want to sign-up with the site. However, there is a trial period of 7 days which costs $7. The trial period will help you decide whether to continue with the services of the company or not.

Samples of Advertised Projects (Gofreelance)

See some of the projects posted on gofreelance.com (as at September 2010)

Java Program
The goal of this assignment is to gain practical experience with procedural abstraction and file I/O.

Website Developer for Legal Firm
Looking for a web and tech-savvy computer whiz to create/revamp an international legal website
Job based on Commission

We need someone able to sell our translation services worldwide on commission basis only.

Fashion Design
Making patterns and clothing samples for infant girls brand

Have Technical Aptitude Research Video Games
This is a Rare Opportunity to Work with a Global Leader in Video Game Intellectual Property Rights.

Home-Based Customer Service
Home-Based Customer Service Specialist needed to follow up with existing and new clients. Applicant must be both professional and courteous. Good telephone skills, along with great oral, verbal and written skills. For more information, please e-mail lary.williams@live.com with resume. This position is part-time $500/weekly.

Project Consultant
We are in the very preliminary stages of launching an equity fund using many of the aspects in the funds voting process that are used in online games.

Selling Leadership Training
I am a Human Resource/Training person and need someone to market my product. I am looking for someone who can put "butts in the seats" so I can focus on scheduling/delivering the training.

Webstore Content
Need help writing content for my webstore.

Looking for an English teacher
Dear Teacher, I am from Stockholm, Sweden and work as an Engineer at Dalofa cooperation

international, Nigeria. My friend whom recently joined the company and from Sweden needed an English teacher

Significantly improve my website. I need a person that can redesign my Web page in order to achieve business performance. Experience with HostGator.

PRArticle Writer (Philippines)
PR/Article Writer (Philippines) Location: Marikina City, Philippines Applications: If you think you fit the bill, send your application with attached CV and portfolio to careers@myoptimind.com

PHPMySQL Web-Based Beta Program
We are assisting a client develop a subscriber-driven product/service review website aimed at Latin America that requires strong, stable back-end programming.

It is High Time You Acted?

Aside bidding for projects on freelance websites (not only Gofreelance), you can also render your services via your own website if you wish. Hence, the truth of the matter is that you can enhance your business revenue through the internet.

> *The search for the perfect venture can turn into procrastination. Your idea may or may not have merit. The key is to get started.*
> *- Unknown Author*

With what you have read so far, the questions I put before you at this time are "Will you allow the book in your hand to turn your financial situation around for good"? "Are you willing to make quite a lot of money on the internet"?

If your answers are yes, then you need to get connected to the internet right away and start to create a website (or a blog) for your online business (services) – though this will cost you some amount of money.

So, In a nutshell, it is not what you know that gives you money but what you do with what you know.

With determination to excel and making use of the right tools, you are bound to succeed as you act on what you have read thus far.

In fact, may I tell you that the only hindrance to your success in life is YOU? Your success is in your hand.

The next chapter will teach you how to make money from quality products and also from used items via online auctions.

Until you value yourself you will not value your time. Until you value your time, you will not do anything with it.
- M. Scott Peck

CHAPTER 5

ONLINE INCOME #5

ONLINE AUCTIONS:
Make Money Through Online Auctions

http://www.istockphoto.com/file_thumbview_approve/8217356/2/istockphoto_8217356-kitchen-items.jpg&imgrefurl

Introduction

In the previous chapter, I emphasized on rendering services online - an avenue by which an offline service company could maximize its profits on the internet.

But in this chapter, my emphasis is on selling products on the internet through auctions – both hard and soft/digital products (examples of digital products are e-book, software etc.). For instance, you can sell any downloadable items on the internet.

Using eBay or any other auction sites affords the vendors the opportunity to sell used and abandoned products, and quality products as well to people who are in dire need of them (and are ready to get these products via auctions).

Even used clothes, children toys, old books etc are offered for sale on auction sites. Abandoned materials held in the garage for years could be converted into cash through auctions.

What to Figure Out Before You Sign-up With EBay

First of all, you need to consider the product(s) you intend to sell online - either to sell scraps or high quality products, or both. Aside the above, you have to take into account what your competitors are charging for a similar product. This will help you determine your starting-price. Make sure you sell product that people are looking for. You can do a search on ebay for this. Also, make sure your auction closes between Monday and Thursday (between 9.00 and 11.00pm eastern), and should be run for 7 (seven) days.

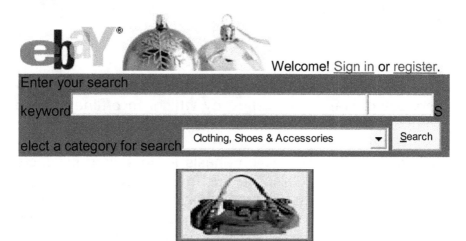

Versace Handbag Purse Leather Italian AUTHENTIC
Current Price: **$1,099.00** *View similar items. ..*
Source: www.ebay.com

After knowing the product to sell (before you spend a dime), you have to take a look on eBay to see what your competitors are offering – the price, and any other things you think will make them have an edge over you. You have to study them, and if necessary replicate what you see on their eBay pages. I don't mean you should take other people's words as if they were your words (plagiarism).

Without any doubt, online auction is one of the avenues people use to make money on the internet. There are websites that run online auctions such as the popular www.eBay.com, one of the best book-selling sites www.amazon.com and a widely known site that gives free email addresses www.yahoo.com.

In addition to the websites above, a site you need to check out is http://www.internetauctionlist.com – a directory of online auction websites.

On any online auction websites, each product is normally sold to the highest bidder and virtually all products could be purchased there. People sell whatever stuff they have and cash in money in turn. To make huge profits one could sell items that have high mark-up (expressing profit as a percentage of cost price). Getting 500% or more mark-up on cost is absolutely possible when you auction digital products such as video CD, ebook. These products cost less to produce and yield good returns on investment than the physical (hard) ones.

Whenever you place an item for auction, it is expected that you (the person who is offering an item for sale) will send the item to whosoever wins the bid while the person who wins the bid is also expected to pay for it.

When the auction expires, which always last for a specific period of time - three, seven or perhaps ten days, the winner of the auction (the person with the highest bid) is expected to pay for the item, including any attendant expenses such as shipping expenses, through an identified means of payment (online payment).

After being paid, the seller is expected to forward the item to the buyer. Auction always starts with a pre-determined price set by the seller before people start to bid on it.

Moreover, there are two types of online auctions operating online. They are general and the specialized auctions. While the general auction is wide in scope in terms of products people sell there (virtually all products), the latter deals with specialized products.

EBay (the most popular auction site) charges a little fee for listing a product and a percentage commission after the sale of the product.

However, knowing what to sell is one thing, selling the same to your intending buyers is another thing entirely. So, you have to come up with an appealing advertising description (for your ebay's product) that will make people who see your advertisement fall in love with your product(s).

To get this done, you can replicate any successful ad. In fact, anything that will make your ad look attractive and appealing should be added – you may add graphic or special colour to your advert to get the needed attention (anything you think will make people to click on your ad).

Check this site for software that will help you create an appealing advert for your eBay.
http://www.auctionriches.com/vadpro.htm

Even if you are on the right track, you will get run over if you just sit there.
- Will Rogers

Using EBay to Promote Your Website

One critical issue you need to know on the internet is how to use an income making technique to create more income for yourself. If you cogitate and explore the internet, you will discover how to use one money making strategy to create another income stream (or multiple streams of online income).

Do you know you can use eBay to promote your website by linking your eBay page to it (site), and even sell at a higher price? Once you do not contravene the rules and the regulations of EBay, you are free to do so. EBay allows anyone to link to his sites (from eBay) provided he is willing to sell at a price higher than the one listed on eBay (for the same item).

Superb Customer Care is Essential

At this point, I will like to say that your online business success is not hinged on having attractive advertisement(s), you must ensure that your customer service is superb. If you treat your customers very well, you are likely to earn more. Superb customer service will lead to recurring sales – the bottom line is that more profits will be earned. Thus, having excellent customer care is essential to your business success.

If you don't take good care of them there is a tendency for your customers to patronize another business. They may even use the "word of mouth marketing" to ruin your business to some extent.

For instance, you need to tell the bidders beforehand, through your advert, the shipping method you intend to use – either courier or postal agency. The shipping and handling costs must also be communicated to them before they bid. There won't be any complaint if this information is related to them at the appropriate time.

> ### Unless you try to do something beyond what you have already mastered you will never grow. - Ronald. E. Osborn

Flexible Payment Options

This is an important issue that calls for serious consideration. If your online payment is restricted to Paypal, MasterCard and VisaCard, you will definitely lose some prospective bidders. They will not bid for your items if they don't have any of the payment options above.

That is just the reason why you have to be flexible in your payment options. You may add the following payment options to make payment more flexible – checks, eBay bill point, money order and cash by mail. With this, more people are going to bid for your items. Focusing on Paypal is niece since the same (Paypal) is owned by ebay, but adding other payment options will boost your sales.

Making Your Advert Description Stand Out

To drive traffic to your eBay page, you have to figure out kinds of keywords you expect people looking for the products you are selling to search for. If you are able to figure out this, you are likely to come up with relevant keywords for your advert description.

Your advertisement should include essential wordings that will attract people to it. You may add symbols to your description as well.

Creating About Me Page

Creating "About Me Page" may add value to your online auction business. With about me page, people get to know the products you are offering for sale, and your personal information such as hobbies, careers and the like. You may add your photograph if you wish. However, prior to the time of creating "About Me Page", make sure you read through the guidelines so as to do what is expected of you.

Aside this, a signature file which entails your website link, should be provided at the bottom of your "About Me Page" to enable people visit your site, and buy your product.

In chapter 6, I will coach you how to cash in money on the internet with a digital camera.

It is time to break through the barriers that have held you back and held you down for such a long time. It is time to reach out and indelibly etch your place in history. - Greg Hickman

CHAPTER 6

ONLINE INCOME #6

DIGITAL PHOTOGRAPHS:
Make Money Selling Digital Photos

http://motherlandnigeria.com/pictures.html

Introduction

Not many people know they can make money selling digital photos on the internet. Perhaps, you have just discovered this yourself, then you need to take advantage of reading this book to enhance your earnings. You don't have to be educated (or possess good writing skills), which is the pre-requisite for rendering specialized consulting services, before you profit from digital photos.

> *To accomplish great things*
> *we must first dream, then*
> *visualize, then plan...*
> *believe... act!*
> *- Alfred A. Montapert*

Oftentimes, people snap pictures just for fun without realizing the possibility of converting the same into money – that's selling their pictures at photo gallery websites. No wonder they stock their cell phones with diverse shots which yield no financial gain. Did you take pictures of late? If yes, did you profit from them? Why can't you turn your pictures into a business venture? Why can't you make money from something you love with passion?

Yes, you can! You can make money from your hobby if you wish. Selling digital photos is indeed one of the ways of earning income online, and you need no special training before making money from photos. All you need to do is take a shot and place it online for sale.

However, anyone who is willing to make money from this business must acquire a digital camera for taking assorted photographs, and equally have access to the internet to make uploading of images possible.

While special training is not compulsory, it is, however, essential that you have access to some key information that will enhance your earnings. That is you need to know the right keyword(s) to use. Through Yahoo, Google, Bing or any other popular search engines you can generate keywords for your images. You can as well, if you desire, visit CameraDollar.com for Camera dollars income system. This site may teach you all you need to know about making money with digital photos – though for a fee.

http://www.cp-africa.com/wp-
content/uploads/2010/07/cpafrica1.jpg&imgrefurl

Going Part-Time or Full-Time: The Choice is Yours!

You will obviously earn money when your pictures are sold on any of the photo gallery websites. What you intend to achieve in terms of financial reward, and probably, the time at your disposal will surely determine your career path – whether to go full time or part time. The choice is yours!

Whichever career path you choose to follow, you still need to add one or two online money making techniques to selling digital photos in order to enhance your income because selling digital photos alone on the internet may not earn you huge amount of money (**I do not advise you to sell any pornographic pictures**). To enhance your income, you may add affiliate marketing programme, Google Adsense or any other money making technique(s) you have read so far (or you are about to read).

Generate Money through Unrestricted Uploaded Shots and Referral Programme

The upside of selling digital photos is that a shot can be downloaded as many times as possible. This will invariably increase your earnings as many diverse pictures are uploaded (many shots of different identities). Since you have no limit to the number of shots of different identities you could upload, the possibility of making a reasonable amount of money is evident.

You can also enhance your earnings by helping the photos gallery websites sell more through referral programme. You get paid when someone signs up through you. So, your income will increase as you get more people to sign up. With this, you will be able to generate income from both ways – make money selling digital photos and from referral programme.

Photo Gallery Websites

You can register with any of these photo gallery websites and start, in earnest, to upload your pictures for sale.

www.crestock.com

www.ktools.net

www.stockandprints.com

www.istockphoto.com

www.foliolink.com

www.morephotos.com

www.photostockplus.com

www.shutterstock.com

http://www.turkishairlines.com/images/skylife/8-2006/116/14_116lagos%2520island%2520from%2520theC2624.jpg&imgrefurl

Importance of Adherence to Content Guidelines

However, before you register with any of the above websites (or perhaps any websites not mentioned in this book), it is important you familiarize yourself with the content guidelines of these websites (or better still the terms of service). You need to be aware of any prohibited images and the ones (images or videos) these sites accept. It is unreasonable for you to upload to a site an image that contravenes the terms of service of that website. For instance, shutterstock.com does not allow its subscribers to upload images they do not own (images not created by them) to its website. Therefore, prospective subscribers should ensure that whatever images (or videos) they are uploading are created by them.

> *The will to win, the desire to succeed, the urge to reach your full potential... these are the keys that will unlock the door to personal excellence. - Eddie Robinson*

Frequently Asked Questions (FAQ) Section – ... Important Place to Visit

In addition to the above, you should visit the FAQ section of each one of these sites to get additional information about their services. Through Frequently Asked Questions (FAQ) section, you will know what you ought to do (and what you are not expected to do).

Having sound knowledge of what these sites offer – that's to know what they want and what they dislike, will be of great help to you. It helps you know what their content guidelines are and the types of images you can upload to such sites. Your visit to these sites will also help you to avoid warning as a result of flaws (content flaws).

Shutterstock.com Frequently Asked Questions (FAQ) - Please Visit this Site for Details

Can I join if I am outside the USA?

Yes! Certain high fraud areas of the world may require prior approval before an account is created. If your country isn't listed on the signup form, please contact support and submit your portfolio. We may also require references. As long as you can receive and cash checks by air postal mail, and your pictures are 100% yours, you can join. Checks will be drawn in US dollars - so make sure your bank is capable of cashing this type of check.

How is editorial stock different from commercial stock?

Commercial stock images are used in advertisements, promotions, and anything that would endorse a product or service. Editorial stock is a newsworthy account of events.

While we cannot guarantee that this will always be true, commercial designers will NOT be able to use your image. Your image will only be used by newspapers, magazines, TV, and other news organizations that aren't endorsing a product or service.

What is a $.05 download?

Shutterstock subscribers have the option of asking us to back up the photos they have downloaded during their subscription onto a CD. We mail this CD to them at the end of each month. When they choose this option, we pay those who have submitted an additional $.05 per image -- this is our way of giving incentive to people to participate in the CD backup program. They are free to opt in or out of the CD backup program at anytime.

What if I don't receive payment?

Payments don't go out till mid-month. Checks can take up to 4 weeks to arrive at their destination and 6 weeks if sent internationally. If you still do not receive your check six weeks after the end of the calendar month, please contact support and we will send you a new check. We can only reissue payment in the original form of payout.

What is a warning?

A warning puts you on notice that a large percentage of your images contain flaws. The most common problem is noise in the images. Be sure to check your work at 100%.

Here are some more common reasons people get warnings:
1. Submitting more than one of the same image
2. Keyword spamming (using the same keywords for unlike images)
3. Frequent not categorized
4. Large numbers of out-of-focus or noisy photos in a batch
5. Submitting an image that has already been rejected without leaving a note for the reviewer as to why it was resubmitted
6. Multiple combinations of images with problems (i.e. poor framing, focus, key wording, etc. all in the same batch)
7. Upsizing of images more than 5%
8. Large batches (over 50) with all poor quality shots (this includes not rotated images, snapshots, noise, etc.)

Please see the Submitter Guidelines for additional detail on this.

How much will I be paid as a submitter?

Our current payout rate for Standard License 25-A-Day Subscription downloads is: $.25 (25 cents per image download). After earning a total of $500, your rate increases to $.33 per download. Once you surpass a total lifetime earnings of $3,000, your rate will increase to $.36 per download, and after you reach $10,000 in lifetime earnings, your rate will increase to $.38 per download.

Our current payout rate for On Demand Subscription downloads is: $.81 for the Small/Medium Image Size plan, and $1.88 for the All Sizes plan. After earning a total of $500, the rate increases to $1.07 per download for Small/Medium and $2.48 for all sizes. Once you surpass a total lifetime earnings of $3,000, your rate will increase to $1.17 for Small/Medium and $2.70 for all sizes. After you reach $10,000 in lifetime earnings, your rate will increase to $1.24 for Small/Medium and $2.85 for all sizes.

Additionally, the royalty for an Enhanced License image download is $28.

At 25 cents per download, how am I going to make any money?

Shutterstock is a subscription-based stock library. Buyers may download a few hundred pictures in a single month's membership. We get a wide variety of users subscribing, so the more images you have in our library, the more you can make!

The $0.25 per download payout adds up fast - for example, if your images are downloaded 1000 times over the course of a month, you will receive $250 for that month! And after earning a total of $500, your rate will increase to $0.33 per download, with a tiered set of pay increases as you reach the $3,000 and $10,000 milestones. If you make $250 per month, that's $3000 per year from images that would normally be collecting dust on your hard disk!

Where else will my photos be sold?
Photos will be sold from our main Shutterstock.com website - http://www.shutterstock.com/. Some affiliates may sell our photos also though a co-branded site - you will be paid for all downloads resulting from these co-branded sites as well.

Does it cost anything to become a submitter?
No -- We want to pay you! It's free to contribute, and you will get paid each time your content is downloaded.

I am currently selling my content on other sites - is this OK?
Yes. Shutterstock's Submit Terms of Service is not exclusive; therefore, you may also submit to other agencies.

The indispensable first step to getting the things you want out of life is this: decide what you want. - Ben Stein

---

Can I add extra keywords to my images just so they will show up in more searches?
You are responsible for choosing keywords for your own images, but we do not recommend using a thesaurus, and keyword-spamming (using unrelated words) in order to be included in more searches is against our Submitter rules. We will disable your account if we find out that you are keyword-spamming. Please see our

Submitter Guidelines for clarity on this and other related submitter policies.

Is there a minimum payout?

Yes, you must accumulate at least $75 to be paid by Paypal or Moneybookers, or $300 to be paid by paper check. All earnings are brought forward into the next pay period until you reach the minimum, at which time a payout will be issued automatically. If you close your account before your earnings reach the minimum, you will forfeit those earnings. The default minimum payout is set to $100 - you can change it to $75 if you would like within the 'My Account' part of the website.

How often will I be paid?

Monthly, checks are sent out for the previous month's payouts. For example: On the 15th of March, payments will be sent for February downloads. If during any period you haven't reached the minimum payout, your earnings will be brought forward to the next pay period.

Do I need to request a payout?

No - once you reach the minimum earnings amount for your payment type, a check or e-payment will automatically be processed. Please make sure we have accurate information so that payments aren't delayed. You may set your minimum payout to be as low as $75 for Paypal or Moneybookers payments.

Can I change keywords after I upload a photo?

Yes - you can. Simply go to your list of approved or pending photos, and click on the pencil icon. Any modifications to the description, categories, or keywords, will result in the re-queuing of your photo for approval.

http://planetejeanjaures.free.fr/geo/afrique/nigeria2.ht
m

Digital photos: Earn More Selling Photos on Many Websites

The best way to enhance your earnings is to register with many websites as possible. With this, you are sure of making more money when your digital photos are sold on these gallery websites.

Let's use the hypothetical example below to illustrate how to make more money selling digital photos:

Let's assume you uploaded a picture (a shot) to eight gallery websites selling digital photos. Supposing your image was downloaded 100 times on each one of the sites (getting 800 downloads from eight websites) and the payout rate per download was 25 cents or $0.25 (on each one of the gallery websites). With the above scenario, you would earn $200 from a shot/photo (not even two pictures).

Furthermore, assuming you uploaded another four images on each one of these photo gallery sites, and all the images were downloaded hundred times on each site (assuming the payout rate was still $0.25), then you would earn $800. Of course, that is a reasonable amount of money!

Having come to the end of this chapter - **DIGITAL PHOTOGRAPHS, Make Money Selling Digital Photos**, you need to act right away if this chapter is of interest to you.

You will learn how to make money filling survey forms, and entering data in the next chapter

**Decide what you want
decide what you are
willing to exchange for it.
Establish your priorities
and go to work.
- H. L. Hunt**

CHAPTER 7

ONLINE INCOME #7

DATA ENTRY:
Make Money Entering Online Data For Companies

http://www.defectivebabyproducts.com/images/child que.jpg&imgrefurl

Make Money by Taking Part in Online Surveys

Online survey is one of the ways of making money on the internet. You can partake in this and make a decent amount of money. Online survey makes it possible for people to get extra money by filling in surveys (and answering questionnaires) from companies that are looking for honest opinion in regard to their products. It might take you few hours of work per week, but you will get paid if you take part. Your earnings per week might not even be substantial (maybe $50 a week), but is still worth considering if you are sure of getting the same amount of money on a weekly basis.

The beauty of online survey is that you need not to buy any product. It may cost you nothing or little amount of money to get started. Your earnings will be determined by your efforts and how often you take part in surveys. If you take time to do a search on the internet, you will discover a few companies that offer real online surveys.

> *Those who dare to fail greatly can ever achieve greatly.*
> *- Robert F. Kennedy*

Please beware! Not all the websites promoting surveys and data entry work are genuine sites. In fact, many are not genuine especially those that say, you are in for huge earnings when you register with them. They are just looking for a way to siphoning your hard earned money through a deceptive advertisement. That is why you have to be very careful and carry out a thorough research work before you part with your money.

However, any survey website could restrict participation in surveys to any countries (to the citizens and residents of such countries) of its choice. For instance, a site can restrict participation to the citizens (or residents) of the United States of America (USA) and Canada will not allow people residing in Africa or any other parts of the world to participate in its surveys.

It is the policy of Gofreelance to send periodical surveys to its members and prospects alike through their (members and customers) email addresses. You will get jobs posted to you if you sign up with the site.

Samples of surveys on Gofreelance.com (previously advertised)

Complete Simple Surveys from Home: An expanding company is looking for freelancers to help with market research from home. You will be required to complete short surveys and provide answers to questions on various products.

Complete Simple Surveys from Home: A market research company is seeking people who can undertake surveys from home to evaluate various products. You must have a good Internet connection and speak fluent English

Make Money Sorting Emails, Entering Resumes into Databases, and Posting Job Openings

Aside online survey, you can as well make a reasonable sum of money by entering data into companies' databases (computers). Some companies do outsource their offline data entry work to data entry service providers. You can actually earn a handsome amount of money by entering data entry forms (or filling in data entry forms) if you know the sites that offer such. You can check out the following sites www.digitalpoint.com and www.sitepoint.com for data entry jobs. It costs you nothing to fill a data entry form, but you have to be smart to be the first to spot any data entry jobs on these sites.

You may also visit www.elance.com for data entry jobs. See underneath an advertisement on data research and data entry on elance.com site (www.elance.com)

Posted: Mon, Dec 20, 2010
Time Left: 12d, 18h
Location: Anywhere
Start: Immediately
Budget: Less than $500
Fixed Price Job
Guaranteed with Elance Escrow
W9 Not Required

We have an ON GOING need for basic Search data research and data entry.
The initial project is for 500 keywords, but we have an ongoing need to research thousands of keywords, therefore, we are looking for a strong, sizable, experience team that can scale with us quickly.
Requirements:

1. Access to your own Google AdWords account
2. Understanding and use of proxy servers
3. Ability to install and use Tor proxy server
4. A large, experienced research and data entry team, experienced in Search key phrase research
5. References for previous large scale data entry projects

Only bid if you:
1. Have proven experience and references handing large scale

data entry projects
2. Have your own Adwords account, and are very familiar with the keyword tool, and Search research
3. Understand how to use proxy servers
4. Can ultimately handle thousands of keyword research items each week
Process:
For each keyword in the attached spreadsheet, determine the total Google Search results, ...

Gofreelance.com is another website that offers data entry jobs. See underneath the samples of data entry jobs (previously advertised) on Gofreelance.com. Note that you can only take part in any of the projects (jobs on gofreelance.com) when you register with the site and pay a monthly subscription of $49.95 {or make a trial payment of $7 for seven (7) days}. You may decide to continue with the services of this site after seven (7) day trial period.

Home Based Data Entry Assistant Required: A fast-growing consumer goods company is looking for a home-based assistant who can undertake a range of data entry tasks. You must speak good English and have access to the Internet.

Filter Email for a Busy Executive ($700.00 per week): A high-profile executive with a crowded inbox is seeking a virtual assistant who can go through email daily and deal with non-mission critical messages. You will filter out junk mail, reply to straightforward inquiries and forward important messages for executive attention.

Data Entry Email Handling -Work from your home full or part-time. - Complete on-line training included -You are paid for most every response you send. Work at your convenience.

Data Entry Work

You can check out the following sites for data entry work:
http://forums.digital.com
http://sitepoint.com

Steps to Getting Data Entry Work on DigitalPoint.com

1. You need to first of all sign-up with the website before you look for data entry jobs
2. After you have set-up a forum account with the site, then pay a visit to the website's forum page
3. when you get there click on "visit sell, buy or trade forum" link

Steps to Getting Data Entry Work on SitePoint.com

1. You get started by registering a forum account with sitepoint.com
2. After that, you visit the forum page and click on "looking for hire" section of the website

Tips to Getting Data Entry ...

The information below is important to getting data entry jobs at both digital point and site point:

1. Make sure your signature file entails important information such as your website link, email address, your name and telephone number and any other vital contact information. You may do this at the time of signing-up for forum accounts with the two sites
2. Watch the way people respond to post sent by the webmaster whenever a data entry work is available

3. Do not respond to the post without finding out if it is appropriate for you to respond
4. Endeavour to ask question(s) on any issue(s) that is/are unclear to you
5. You may contact one of the forum members for help via personal message
6. Have a right mindset that the job will come to you.
7. Make sure you respond immediately to any treat for data entry job posted by the webmaster
8. Finally, make sure you are the first to spot the data entry job(s) and act immediately.

In the next chapter, you will discover how to enhance your business revenue by selling hard products (physical products), and how to sell physical products on the internet without any inventory.

Give to us clear vision that we may know where to stand and what to stand for because unless we stand for something, we shall fall for anything.
- Peter Marshall

CHAPTER 8

ONLINE INCOME #8

MAKE MONEY SELLING PHYSICAL PRODUCTS (HARD GOODS)

http://www.dhgate.com/promotion/all/Christmas-channel/competition.html#nhpa-mban-1

Hard Products (Hard Goods)

Aside using the internet to sell digital products such as ebooks, photographs etc., it is equally used to sell manufactured products – physical goods. So, the manufacturers, wholesalers and the retailers of physical products can benefit from the wheel of internet technology. Internet has not only served as a source of promoting products (and invariably businesses) but also an avenue of generating substantial amounts of revenue – profits that keep coming year in, year out (that is residual income). That is the bottom line of having a business on the internet.

It is quite unfortunate that there are individuals who are yet to discover how to sky-rocket their earnings/revenues via the internet. Also, there are people who do not believe this is possible in the first place.

Perhaps, you have just discovered this salient fact yourself as a result of reading this book – I congratulate you for getting a copy of this book. However, you must understand you need not to procrastinate (procrastination will take you to nowhere – in fact, it's going to be an obstacle to your success). Thus, whatever knowledge you've acquired from this book, you will only enhance your earnings/revenue if you act on them.

You can enhance your revenue generation (whatever hard products you are selling such as computers, electrical appliances, electronic gadgets, furniture materials, motor vehicles etc.) by taking your business to the internet. Internet is a big market (online market) that covers every nook and cranny of this world. Indeed, it is not only an avenue of selling hard products but also a platform that enables people/organizations minimize their running or business expenses unlike the offline market.

For instance, a drug manufacturing company can generate more revenue via website (with two pages set aside for online payment and thank you message). Each one of the pages on the website (aside those mentioned above, and the following pages such as home page, frequently asked questions page – FAQ page, contact us page and other vital pages depending on what the company wants) is used to promote the company's products – specifically create a web page for each drug (product) the company is offering for sale.

A company that sells a variety of drugs says – 20 varieties of drugs for instance, might create a website of thirty or more pages.

The home page ought to have a table of contents (as a navigational webpage) so that any persons can easily navigate to any page(s) of his/her choice. So, when a prospect clicks on one of the links (or a product symbol) that appears on the home page, he is directed immediately to the product page on the website – the page that gives further information on the product. Also, each one of the pages should be linked to the home page. In addition, each one of the pages (for drugs now) ought to reveal the benefits the buyers/users will derive from the product.

If a prospect makes up his mind to buy any of the products (any of the drugs), after reading through the product's features and benefits, he clicks on one of the payment options (buttons) below the product page - this will enable him fill in an online payment form.

After completing the form which entails payment details such as name, debit card number etc, the prospect clicks on submit button in an attempt to submit the payment form – a click on submit button will facilitate the processing of the form.

Subsequently, a "thank you page" is displayed on the screen – a means of thanking the prospect for taking decision to buy your product. That is the essence of this page.

You can check out this site www.amazon.com – a website that specializes in selling digital and hard books (print materials) online - for different kinds of hard products displayed on the site.

Amazon.com has huge storage capacity to house a lot of books on the internet. That shows you the power of the internet. Really, with internet technology, the possibility of minimizing your marketing expenses is high.

Also, check out this site for hard products www.vstore.ca

My great concern is not whether you have failed, but whether you are content with your failure.
- Abraham Lincoln

The following websites allow you to sell their products on your blog (weblog). They handle orders, payments and products shipments, and it costs you nothing (you pay nothing) to join. The membership is free. However, It is your responsibility, after you have signed up, to sell their products in exchange for a pre-determined percentage commission – (this is applicable to www.zazzle.com); or you set your own mark-up for the products (or any of the products) you have chosen to sell [mark-up is the difference between the cost of producing a product (cost price) and the price it is sold at (selling price)].

www.cafepress.com
www.printfection.com.

Internet Drop Shipping Business

Introduction

Another way to profit from hard goods/physical products is by setting-up an online drop shipping business. This is ideal for people who intend to own online shops without manufacturing any products. With online drop shipping business you don't have to keep inventory of hard goods (or build a warehouse).

You just have to create an online shop to sell other people's products – that is to resell company's products for profits. All you need to do is place an order for any product you want your drop shipping company send to your customer on your behalf. On receiving your order the drop shipping company send the requested products in your business name and your office address to your customers - without him/her (your customer) knowing where the product comes from.

It is pertinent that you take the following factors into consideration before setting-up a drop shipping business:

1. Decide what to sell

Before you venture into a drop shipping business, you first of all decide on the product you want to sell. That is how to start out. Also, you need to figure out your expected earnings or profit from the product (huge or little percentage of the profit you envisage to make).

2. Researching the internet for a reliable drop shipping company

After knowing the product(s) to sell, say computer for instance, you need to consider (this is a crucial decision) how to get a reliable company that will help you drop ship it to your customers. This is one of the things that will determine your success in this business – whether you will make it or not. You can do a search on Google or visit these sites www.wholesalecenter.com/dropshippers.html and www.thomasregister.com for a good number of drop shipping companies.

You have to spend valuable time to conduct a thorough research work if you are serious about making money via drop shipping business. Get to know each of the companies' customer service. Are they superb? Also, ask questions in relation to drop shipping business. Do they have any experience of drop shipping the product you have decided to sell? What about their financials? This is an aspect of business you must not joke with. Financial report tells a lot about a company – if a company will stand the test of time (either economic or financial crises). A company with a strong financial report is likely to keep operating in many years to come. This is not the only criterion for knowing a good company, but obviously one of the criteria you cannot overlook if you want to succeed.

ATMA LUBRICANTS & SPECIALITIES LTD.
Processors & Blenders of Automotive, Industrial Lubricants & Speciality Oil
Regd. Off & Factory : 54-5-41, Plot No. 169, 170, 5th Road, AUTONAGAR, VIJAYAWADA-520007
Grams : ATMA, Phone: 0866 - 2543580, 2544491, , E-mail : vjwatma@sancharnet.in
Mobile : 98481 – 91278   (AN ISO-9001 COMPANY)   Visit us at : www.atmalubricants.org

BUSINESS ASSOCIATE FEED BACK FORM	Ref. No. MKG / QF / 0718 Rev.No. 01 Date : 15.11.2003 Page No. 1 of 1	FOR OFFICE USE ONLY S. No. : Date : Area Code:

NAME :
COMPANY NAME :
PROPRIETOR / PARTNER :
TELEPHONE :
MOBILE :

ADDRESS :
CITY : _____ PIN: _____
E - MAIL :

We do request you to kindly spare a few moments and fill in the Enquiry Form.
The information you provide will help us to understand you better as our prospective Business Associate.
Please mail this form to Atma Lubrics and Specialities Limited.

1) When was your company established? _____

2) The business nature of your company:
   a) C&F agent [ ]   b) Distributor [ ]   c) Consignment agent [ ]
   d) Re-distribution stockist [ ]   e) Wholesaler [ ]   f) Authorised dealer [ ]
   g) Retailer / Dealer [ ]

3) Name the Products you deal in _____

4) Area of your operation:
   a) Local [ ]   b) City/town [ ]   c) District [ ]   d) State [ ]

5) Your turnover in the current financial year Rs (in Lakhs) _____
   (Enclosed last two years sales tax assessment orders and APGST registration certificate)

6) Turnover target for the coming financial year Rs (in Lakhs) _____

7) Do you wish to become a business associate of Atma?
   a) Yes [ ]   b) No [ ]

8) If yes, in which status would you like to join
   a) Consignment Agent [ ]   c) Wholesaler [ ]   d) Liaison agent [ ]   e) Re-Distribution stockiest [ ]
   f) Dealer [ ]

9) Please mention in which city/district/zone would you like to operate _____

10) Your expected monthly turnover from ALSL In Lakhs_____

11) Proposed amount of investment in the business with ALSL
    a) 10 - 20 Lakhs [ ]   b) 5 - 10 Lakhs [ ]   c) 2.5 - 5 Lakhs [ ]   d) 1 - 2 Lakhs [ ]

12) Networking skills
    a) Fairly good [ ]   b) good [ ]   c) Very good [ ]   d) Excellent [ ]

13) Influential skills
    a) Fairly good [ ]   b) good [ ]   c) Very good [ ]   d) Excellent [ ]

14) Business skills
    a) Fairly good [ ]   b) good [ ]   c) Very good [ ]   d) Excellent [ ]

15) Expected ROI (Return on Investment)
    a) 12 - 18 % [ ]   b) 18 - 30 % [ ]   c) 30 - 48 % [ ]

16. Mention three reasons for opting Business Association with ATMA.
    1._____   2._____   3._____

17. Existing infrastructure
    1. Go down   SIZE_____   2. Sales Man   Name, Age and Qualification
    3. Goods Vehicle [Auto] [LCV]_____   4. Office Assistant Name, Age and Qualification.
    5. Own vehicle

http://www.atmalubricants.com/images/FeedbackForm.gif&imgrefurl

You need to find out how much the product(s) you intend to drop ship will cost you, including shipping expenses, so as to determine your profit; and also make sure that your drop-shipping company sells high quality products in order to avoid the product being returned often to them.

3. Setting-up account with the drop shipping company

Having got the company that will help you drop ship computer to your customers, you have to contact this company and set up a reseller account with them. The reseller application may be filled online or offline, and some business documents may be requested for by your drop shipping company to make sure that they are dealing with a legitimate company (since they are the one to send the product {computer for example} to your customer).

4. Advertise the product on auction websites (or on your own online shop)

If you do not have an online shop, you can place an advertisement on eBay (www.ebay.com) or an auction website below:

www.yahoo.com.

It may even be any other auction websites not mentioned in this book.

Whichever auction website you intend to use, you have to determine your opening price (after all, you have known the total cost of buying and shipping the product to your prospects), which must not be less than the total cost of the product including shipping expenses. Assuming the total cost of the product is $200 (including the cost of shipping the product to your customer), and the product sells for any price above $200. The bottom line is that you are making a profit on the product.

You may also sell the product on your online shop, if you have one, and even make more money if the product is sold at a price higher than the one on ebay. Of course, it ought to be higher if you don't want to contravene eBay's laid down rules and regulations (except you don't have account with EBay).

5. Online payment processing systems

The online payment options you intend to use will determine how fast you get paid when your product is sold. Since the time you receive payment will determine not only when an order will be initiated, but also when the product will be sent; it is therefore essential that you use fast payment processing systems so as to place order in good time. PayPal, MasterCard and VisaCard are some of the fastest payment options you could go for.

Throughout the centuries there were men who took first steps, down new roads, armed with nothing but their own vision.
- Ayn Rand

---

6. Order for the product

The moment you get paid for the product (image of the product displayed on your online shop or any of the auction websites), you have to contact your drop shipping company and place an order with them so that the hard product could be sent to your prospects/customers using your business name and your office address. With this, your customer will not know that the product is not coming from you.

7. Do a thorough follow up

This step is very crucial to your success because if your order is not honoured (the product is not sent to your customer), you will be held responsible and this could mar your reputation. That is why you have to follow up your order until you are sure the product has been delivered - your customer has got what he/she paid for. You are not through with your customer until the product gets to his/her hand. As you thoroughly follow-up your drop shipping company and your customer, you will know when the product will be sent and when the same will get to your customer. So, never think you have nothing to do after you have ordered for a product - you need to keep making regular contact with both parties (your customer and your drop shipping company).

Finally, in order to get a satisfactory customer service, you have to deal with a reputable drop shipping company – one that has a name to protect. A company that spent years to build a reputable name will be careful not to put it into sludge.

You will succeed on the internet if you believe in your capability (your natural talents) even if you have no internet knowledge at the moment.

You can make more money selling advertising space online. Join me in the next chapter to see how it works.

Nothing is a waste of time if you use the experience wisely.
- Auguste Rodin

CHAPTER 9

ONLINE INCOME #9

SELLING ADVERTISING SPACE

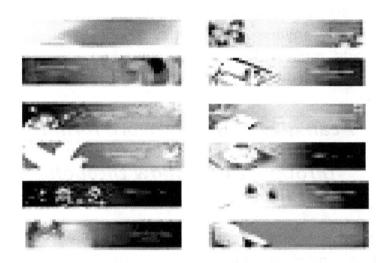

http://www.freeiconsdownload.com/site-images/Large/banner_03.jpg&imgrefurl

Getting Traffic to Your Portal Website

Have you ever seen a banner ad (an abbreviation for advertisement) being displayed on yahoo's site before? Of course, there is a reason why companies always put ads on popular websites such as Google, Bing and Yahoo?

Anyway, the reason is not far-fetched. They are actually looking for traffic (people) they will drive to their websites. Thus, by placing ads on popular websites – sites that not only have reputation, but also generate huge amounts of traffic on a daily basis - they are going to get a large number of people visiting their websites.

It is an indication that anyone could make money selling advertising space on the internet. However, one critical issue anyone going into this kind of business - selling ads, must consider before spending a dime is the issue of traffic (getting people to visit his/her site).

I can give you a six-word formula for success: Think things through, then follow through.
- Captain Edward V. Rickenbacker

To start this business, the first thing you have to do is create a portal website – a website that generates money through sale of advertising space - and afterward you drive traffic to the site. You will get traffic if you are willing to give free materials (including access to free information) to people. People love free stuff such as free ebooks, reports or anything valuable. When valuable materials are given away (free of charge) … the bottom line is that you get a lot of traffic (lots of traffic indeed).

So, you have to build traffic through valuable content and free stuff before you begin to monetize your site after you have generated a large number of subscribers – considerable numbers of people visiting your site. That is the secret of making residual income on the internet.

How to Profit from Traffic

After you have got your portal website filled with a lot of traffic (though this might take you months to achieve) through valuable content and free stuff (and you keep pre-selling your subscribers with valuable content); then you need to consider how to sell advertising space on it (your site). All you need to do is get some companies to advertise their products on your website. Some online companies will pay you huge amounts of money if you have huge numbers of traffic that is related to their niche market – traffic that will sky-rocket their (these companies) revenue (profits).

Aside selling advertising space, you can also sell other people's products (or your own products) on your website in order to increase your revenue generation. You may create an ebook that relates to your site's content for sale.

In addition to the above, you can equally make money from referral fees.

> *Four steps to achievement:*
> *Plan purposefully. Prepare prayerfully. Proceed positively. Pursue persistently.*
> *- William A. Ward*

Measuring Your Website Statistics

Measuring your site audience is essential to achieving your optimum performance. You would not know the number of visitors coming to each one of your website's pages if you are not tracking your website's traffic. Tracking your audience will help you in a great way to knowing the pages that are not attracting high traffic, and taking the necessary steps to improve on such.

It's good if traffic tracking feature comes with your web hosting package so that you need not incur any extra expense on it, but if it does not come with your hosting package then you have to get the tracking software online.

The importance of tracking your website's visitors can not be over-emphasized because it helps you to take wise decisions for optimal performance of your online business. Knowing where to put your website content and the quality of your content, and getting profitable ad campaigns are some of the benefits of tracking your traffic.

You may charge between $20 and $30 dollars per month for one classified advertisement. So if you were able to get, for instance, thirty advertisers buying your advertising space every month, depending on the number of visitors your website is generating, you would be making between $600 and $900 every month on advertisements alone.

You can even make more money as your site's traffic increases. Supposing you had over 100,000 subscribers, you could make a substantial amount of revenue selling advertising space to big companies that might be interested in placing advertisements on your site.

By doing the underneath you can also increase your revenue generation:

1. To sell and rent ads on your e-zine (periodic newsletter)

2. To sell and rent banners, solo and classified ads

3. To profit from links – links (for complementary products) coming from your own website to other people's websites.

Join me in the next chapter in an attempt to show you how to turn overlooked assets into cash.

**Chance favors only
the prepared mind.
- Louis Pasteur**

CHAPTER 10

ONLINE INCOME #10

JOINT VENTURES

http://onewebhosting.com/blog/wp-content/uploads/2009/04/wordofmouth_icon.jpg&imgrefurl

Introduction

I t is unfortunate that many people have not discovered how to enhance their revenue via online joint venture. They do not know how to use other people's assets, and their own assets to create wealth. These unnoticed or unknown assets are not utilised because people do not know how valuable they are -

how they could be used to sky-rocket business revenue. Yes, you can add more revenue to your bottom line if you know how to play the game - make the most of these assets.

After all, you are in business to make money, additional money for that matter; therefore, creating extra or additional revenue via online joint venture is something you should concern yourself with (something you should take an interest in).

Turning other person's valuable assets to your advantage simply means making extra money for yourself through other person's customer/client list. This is possible by selling your products to this list through referral arrangement with the owner of the list – either individual or corporate body.

> *Too many people overvalue what they are not and undervalue what they are.*
> *- Malcolm S. Forbes*

All you need to do is get a businessman who is willing to refer your product(s) to his customer base for profits – which means both of you will benefit from the deal. Mind you, this arrangement can only work with complementary products – not competitive ones.

The beauty of this arrangement is that it is a win/win arrangement – both parties win. The endorser, the one who refers his clients/customers to another person's product/service will profit from anticipated sales revenue (for referring his customers/clients to another person's product).

The seller will not only earn revenue from this arrangement but also gain new long-life customers/clients. What a plus (advantage) to gaining new long-life customers!

Let's look at the scenario below to see how money could be generated through this income generating strategy.

Let's assume a textile company had agreed to strike a deal with company A, a dry cleaning outfit, with a customer database of 500 people. The endorser, company A's owner, after accepting the joint venture contractual agreement, sent copies of letter of endorsement to his customers (of 500 customers). Supposing hundred (100) of this customer base (representing 20% of the customer database) took up the offer; and therefore bought 500 yards of guinea brocade, an average of five (5) yards per customer, at a price of $50 per yard.

Assuming the textile company had agreed to pay the endorser, company A's owner, a referral fee of 40% of the anticipated revenue.

Without taking into account the possibility of getting repeat orders from the new customers, the textile company would make $15,000 as sales revenue while the endorser, a dry cleaning company, would earn a referral fee of $10,000 from the same deal. What a win/win situation.

What a man really wants is creative challenge with sufficient skills to bring him within the reach of success so that he may have the expanding joy of achievement. - Fay B. Nash

---

Getting Started ...

1. You get started by looking for a company or an individual with a client base you can show how to generate more money – make sure you don't reveal the secret at this time
2. After that, you write a letter of endorsement and send it to the person you want to show how to generate more money
3. The next thing you need to do after you have sent your letter of endorsement is to follow–up same with email, phone call, and any other positive ways of getting results.
4. Lastly, you ensure that agreement documents are signed by all the people involved in the deal before revealing the secrets.

Note: To avoid being duped make sure you use a non-disclosure letter which states the agreement terms. After that, you could reveal the secrets.

Getting the Right Deals

1. Get a company or business that has customer database in which the customers have cordial business relationship with the company.
2. Get a product you know those customers will be willing to buy

3. Connect a real estate company with a business outfit or company that has a strong business relationship with its customers, and those customers are willing to buy land
4. Refer people to a dry cleaning outfit, and get paid for this arrangement.

However, to get your customers interested in taking decisions to buy make sure that the product/service has unmet need (a problem or problems) to address.

Using the Internet for Joint Venture Deals

1. The first issue you have to address is how to get a product that is selling – which your customers are willing to buy
2. Visit www.alexa.com and download alexa software to your computer system. This software - after downloading it - will give you information (backdrop) on any site you visit such as email address, name of the site's owner and address, and telephone number.
3. Do a search on the internet for any keywords that interest you such as money making, internet marketing etc., which you could use to get the above backdrop information.
4. Write a proposition letter and send it to the website(s) you have searched on the internet.

Essential Guidelines to Writing a Letter of Proposition

1. Use Google search engine (or any search engine) to search for a prospect for your joint venture, and also

endeavour to study what that prospect is offering. With that, you will be able to write a few persuasive introductory sentences (based on information your prospect is giving its own customers/clients) that will grab your prospect to read through your proposition.

2. Write and send via email a letter of proposition to this prospect.
3. Your letter of proposition should state what you represent – the service(s) you intend to render.
4. The next paragraph should entail what the site you visited (your prospect's site) is all about
5. Let your prospect knows that your services can help him boost its profit.
6. Give your phone number to your prospect and be ready to answer your call(s).
7. End the letter of proposition with a superb closing remark that will arouse the interest of your prospect.
8. The following should be added – yours sincerely or faithfully, your name and your contact telephone number(s).

Chapter 11 focuses on how to make money selling internet infrastructures.

CHAPTER 11

ONLINE INCOME #11

MAKE MONEY SELLING/OFFERING INTERNET INFRASTRUCTURES

http://tinyurl.com/ytocrb

One of the major things that makes internet unique is the use of automated devices (which produces the best possible results) such as autoresponder, web hosting, credit card services etc. It is practically impossible to transact business online without using some of these essential internet tools.

In fact, these online tools have tremendously contributed to the growth of commerce on the internet. For instance, ad tracking software helps webmasters track their ad campaigns to see whether they are getting optimal results for their efforts or not. Additionally, without autoresponder you cannot create a mailing list, and the implication of this is that all the prospects that are not making immediate decisions to buy your product(s)/service(s) would never be won (to buy at a time in the future) in the future (except such people revisit your site) since there is no way to follow-up such.

Imagine, if there were not online payment processing services such as MasterCard, VisaCard, and Paypal etc., online business would be impeded since payments have to be made and confirmed (without any instant payment tools) before physical products would be dispatched (or downloadable products would be accessed).

Indeed, it is absolutely impossible for anyone to gain access to information on the internet without website design and web hosting services. If there were not websites internet would not exist.

For this obvious fact, it is worthwhile (a good decision) to build a business around web design and web hosting services.

Of course, there are other indispensable internet tools (infrastructures) such as internet service provider, computer hardware, computer software etc. You cannot even gain access to any website or blog without computer hardware and software. So, both computer hardware and software are even more important than web design and consulting services because it is not possible to design website without these tools (computer hardware and software).

Aside selling internet infrastructures, you can equally set up an online course, via a website and periodic newsletter, to teach people how to use these internet tools.

> **To succeed... you need to find something to hold on to, something to motivate you, something to inspire you.**
> **- Tony Dorsett**

Since some of these essential internet tools are so important to the existence of internet itself, it is worthwhile to profit from them – to build a business around them (or any of them).

Perhaps, you intend to sell computers (hardware), computer software, autoresponder software etc., or you intend to offer/render any of these underside services such as offering website statistics, website design and consulting, credit card services, online training programme etc. to some internet users, you can only achieve these through the help of the internet infrastructures (or some of them).

See the list of some of the internet infrastructures below:

Autoresponder Software
Webhosting Business
Web design and Consulting
Traffic
Online Training Programme
Credit Card Services

Computer Software
Computer Hardware
Shopping Cart
Website Statistics
Internet Service Provider (ISP)

We compiled a rating list of the **top 10 affordable web hosting** in general with the consideration of price, reliability, features, support, and the reputation in the industry in table below.

#	Web Hosting	Price	Band Width	Disk Space	Free Domain	Hosting Review
1	BlueHost	$3.95	Unlimited	Unlimited	1	BlueHost Review
2	HostMonster	$3.95	Unlimited	Unlimited	1	HostMonster Review
3	HostGator	$4.95	Unlimited	Unlimited	0	HostGator Review
4	Justhost	$3.45	Unlimited	Unlimited	1	Justhost Review
5	IXWebHosting	$3.16	Unlimited	Unlimited	1	IXWebHosting Review
6	GoDaddy	$4.79	Unlimited	Unlimited	0	GoDaddy Review
7	Fatcow	$4.83	Unlimited	Unlimited	1	Fatcow Review
8	1&1	$3.99	10GB	300GB	1	1&1 Review
9	HostRocket.com	$4.95	Unlimited	Unlimited	1	HostRocket.com Review

#	Web Hosting	Price	Band Width	Disk Space	Free Domain	Hosting Review
10	iPowerWeb.com	$3.95	Unlimited	Unlimited	1	iPowerWeb.com Review

Restored accounts

Geocities service closed in 2009. We restored most of closed geocities accounts. If your account is on the list and you would like to continue site development you will have to move it to web hosting company of your choice (see **top 10 affordable web hosting** list above).

Figure 11.1 ... Source: www.starbacks.ca

The next chapter will expose you to another money-making technique titled **make money with incentive offers**.

I have about concluded that wealth is a state of mind and that anyone can acquire a wealthy state of mind by thinking rich thoughts.
– Andrew Young

CHAPTER 12

ONLINE INCOME #12

MAKE MONEY WITH INCENTIVE OFFERS

Source:http://www.freefoto.com/images/1210/14/1210
_14_23---Manhattan-Skyline-New-York-

Introduction

Several ways of making money on the internet have been uncovered in this money-making guide (**creating residual internet income**), but I am going to round off with this technique of creating online income – **make money with incentive offers.**

Incentive offers enable people to earn some money through referral programme. This is one of the marketing strategies that big companies employ to promote their products on the internet.

Really, internet has tremendously contributed to the growth of commerce around the world.

However, internet is not without its downside. In fact, it is a technology that exposes people to vices such as watching pornographic pictures, hacking etc (including unproductive time and efforts people expended on the internet all in the name of browsing).

In actual fact, whatever you get on the internet is the by-product of your actions (your thoughts). That is the truth of the matter.

Good, better, best; never let it
rest till your good is better
and your better is best.
- Unknown Author

How to Enhance Your Earnings with Incentive Offers

There are companies that set aside huge amounts of money (as advertising budget) to promote their products via incentive offers on the internet. They pledge to give referral fee to people who refer a specific number of people to their sites.

For instance, a company might promise to give $500 in exchange for fifteen (15) visitors to its site (of course, its product's site). That means you have to refer at least 15 prospects (people) to the company's website if you want to profit from this offer.

All you need to do is visit some forum websites on the internet (if you want to profit from this offer), where you can easily get people to relate with, and pledge to give them some amount of money, say $18 per person, if they sign-up or refer somebody to the site you are promoting. Mind you, you don't have to disclose the name of the company to your prospects.

Assuming you were able to get the required number of people the company is looking for {that is fifteen (15) people signed up for the offer}, then you would make $230 ($500 – $270) via this money making technique.

How do you get paid?

Really, you get paid by setting up a paypal account (or any other acceptable payment option). As soon as the company put $500 into your paypal account, you ensure that those who took part in the promotion are paid forthwith (and you keep the rest).

Finally, you need to commit your time and efforts to this money making technique if you are willing to make a reasonable amount of money.

Take a look at this website www.projectpayday.com

In the next chapter, you will learn how to use internet tools to getting optimal results – getting your messages delivered with less efforts and low costs.

> *We advance on our journey only when we face our goal when we are confident and believe we are going to win out.*
> *– Orison Swett Marden*

CHAPTER 13

ESSENTIAL ONLINE BUSINESS TOOLS:
Must Have Internet Tools For Optimal Results

http://www.pjdesignsandconcepts.com/info/wp-content/uploads/2009/11/webdesign3.jpg&imgrefurl

Introduction

You cannot achieve much on the internet without using the essential online tools. These internet tools are critical to getting optimal performance of your online business. Without them, your internet business (be it affiliate marketing programme, info product etc.) becomes tedious, time consuming, and invariably money wasting.

It would be tedious and energy sapping to send email to hundreds or thousands of people in a day without using autoresponder software. Indeed, it is going to be tedious!

Additionally, it is not only your time and energy that will be consumed, but also cause you to loss prospects, existing customers and money if you transact online business without using these essential tools.

Imagine hundreds or thousands of prospects (including anticipated sales revenue) you are likely to lose if you fail to use autoresponder to gather names and email addresses of people who come across your website.

Our attitude toward life determines life's attitude towards us.
- Earl Nightingale

These online tools include autoresponder software (mentioned above), mailloop, graphic design software, ad tracking software, alexa software, online payment processing tools etc.

Autoresponder Software

This software helps webmasters to reach their prospects (their newsletters' subscribers) with appealing periodic newsletters so as to persuade them to buy their products. The same (autoresponder) could be used to sell back-end products to customers. The beauty of this software is that an email could be sent to hundreds or thousands of people at a time (and newsletters could be sent to prospects and customers alike at regular intervals).

With autoresponder (for sending newsletter), your sequential newsletter or emails are sent to your prospects and/or customers automatically at any predetermined time. All you need to do is write as many emails as you desire and upload them to your autoresponder; and subsequently send them – your newsletter will get to your prospects and customers at regular intervals. This may be once a day, once a week, twice a week or at any time you wish (the number of messages to be sent at your definite time).

www.getresponse.com
www.autoresponder.com
www.robotreply.com
www.sendfree.com
www.aweber.com

You can get your autoresponder service on the internet via any of the websites above if this feature (autoresponder) is not included in your web hosting package.

See underneath some autoresponder websites on the internet and the attendant features:
Free Email Autoresponder Services
Set up automatic replies to your incoming emails

Aweber

Professional autoresponder solution with unlimited follow-up messages, HTML/plain text options, a web form generator, a wide range of HTML email templates, the ability to customize emails with up to 25 fields, and much more. Automated tools to help ensure your emails get delivered and comply with all relevant legislation.

FollowingUp

The free service level is limited to a single autoresponder, 2 messages, and a maximum of 100 subscribers. Several paid upgrades are available that remove these restrictions.

FreeAutoBot

This free autoresponder service lets you send out one or several follow up messages at intervals you specify. No ads are added to your outgoing messages; the site makes money off ads on the main site, and by sending advertising messages to registered users.

Get Response

Free autoresponder service that offers unlimited autoresponders, no maximum mail length, automatic multiple messages sent over a period of time and much more. While the service is free, a short ad is included at the top of every message you send out. You can upgrade to remove the ads, and gain access to more sophisticated, advanced features.

Responders.net

Free autoresponder and form for collecting information on your site. You can set up an information request form easily, and specify what message you would like to send automatically to the people who fill in the form.

SendFree

Autoresponder service with an interesting twist: SendFree also acts like an advertising exchange service. How it works: you sign up for a SendFree account and set up your autoresponder service. At the top of every automatic reply your autoresponder sends out is a short text advertisement. Half of these are for other members' sites. The other own half are reserved for SendFree's advertisers. In turn, your advertisement will appear at the top of messages sent out by other members.

It is good you create your own mailing list software so that no individual will be able to access your mailing list (which is created by this software); but if you do not want to be in control of the list (that means some people could gain access to your mailing list), then you have to build one via any of the third party sites such as aweber, sendfree, etc.

You can get free CGI script on the following websites to help create your own mailing list:

www.cgi-resoucres.com
www.sitepoint.com

This site www.sparklist.com/index/html can help you build a mailing list at a reasonable and affordable fee if you don't have the knowledge of programming language to build one, or perhaps you just don't have time to do it yourself (not that you don't have a wide knowledge of programming language).

Web Design and Web Hosting

If you want to run a successful online business, it is essential that you get a good web hosting company which provides a high quality technical/customer service (24 hrs a day/7 days a week). You might lose your ranking (site) on search engines if your web hosting company's server goes down, and the problem is not solved in good time. In fact, you will not only lose your ranking but also your money (that is the consequence of a sudden dip in ranking). For this reason, you have to do a search for a good web hosting company. Please be wary of those sites that do not offer quality services (including sites that offer free low quality blogs on the internet) if you want to get the best blog, you can visit www.blogger.com or www.wordpress.com.

You can also visit any of the sites below for your web hosting package:
www.hostgator.com
www.ipowerweb.com
www.1&1.com
www.sitebuildit.com
www.godaddy.com
www.bluehost.com,
www.ixwebhosting.com
www.yahoo.com

Keep your thinking right And your business will be right. - Zig Ziglar

---

While you can venture into some online businesses such as affiliate marketing, selling photographs etc. without having a website; however, you will do yourself good if you have a website to promote your business (so, whatever business you intend to do on the internet it is important that you create a website to promote it). If you have knowledge of programming language, of course, you can design the website yourself, and then contact a web hosting company to host it for you. If you can't do it yourself, then entrust the designing and hosting of your site to a web hosting company. Let them do it for you for a fee.

You may as well engage a freelance programmer to help you build your website. You can get a freelance programmer to help you build your website via www.elance.com. If you decide to do it (create a website) yourself, then you can use xsitepro software on www.xsitepro.com even if you don't have knowledge of programming language.

However, before you design and host your site you still have to consider some vital issues. These include the choice of your domain name, your niche market, profitable site concept (profitable keywords), and more importantly, quality content. All these ought to have positive effect on your online business, your ranking (website) on search engines, the quality of your visitors, and the ratio of those (visitors) that make repeat visit(s) to your site to those that do not make repeat visit(s).

You need to figure out your niche market and the people you intend to serve (prospective customers) before you design your website.

Aside the foregoing paragraphs, ensure that your domain name possesses the following criteria.
1. Use a short domain name
2. Make your domain name attractive so that people can click on it. See an example below **www.onlinemoneymaking.com**
3. Make it very simple to remember – a domain name that is easy to remember
4. You should use your domain name to tell people about your products/services

5. Use a domain name that has a relationship with your niche market. If you are selling ebook titled "how to make money online", you may come up with something like **www.onlinemoneymaking.com** as your domain name. This domain name is not available so you cannot use it, please take note.
6. Make your domain name easy to spell

You can use **dot com** as your domain name extension. If your desired domain name has been taken, you can use acronym to form a domain name. You can use acronym GOOD to form a domain name – see this example www.GetOutOfDebt.com. Similarly, this domain name (www.GetOutOfDebt.com) is not available for use – it is an existing site.

If your desired domain name (dot com) is not available, you can use one of these extensions – dot net, dot biz, dot info, dot org (for non-profit making organization) etc.

Online Payment Processing Services

It is good to have more than one online instant payment accounts such as VisaCard, MasterCard, Paypal, Discovery etc on your website. The higher the number of online payment options available on your site to your prospects, the higher the possibility of getting more customers/clients (the lesser the number of online payment options available on your site to your prospects, the higher the likelihood of losing prospective customers/clients to your competitors). So, you may add cash by mail, cheque, wire transfer and money order to your payment options. In a nutshell, you need to make your payment options flexible enough so as to enhance patronage – you stand a chance of getting more patronage by putting five or more payment options on your site.

Getting merchant accounts for your online business transactions might be a herculean task (depending on your country of residence). It would be niece if your web hosting package includes this feature. If not, you have to contact your web hosting company to see how they can help you out. You may as well do a search on the internet for site(s) that offer(s) online payment services.

You may also visit any of the online payment processing websites below:
www.clickbank.com
www.1shoppingcart.com

Mind you, getting clickbank payment processing service will cost you a one-time set up fee approximately $50 (as you can see in page 171).

Additionally, 1shopping cart payment option has a tracking feature, though with a recurring fee. For affiliate marketing programme, I advise you to use 1shopping cart or clickbank as your online instant payment account. However, you have to find out if you (depending on your country of residence) could sign up for their affiliate marketing programme.

PayPal
PayPal is one of the pioneers in the free credit card processing solutions, offering a wide range of options and services. As a

sister company of Ebay, it is a natural choice if you are going to conduct your business on this popular auction site.

Basic features:

Lower transaction fees than other 3rd party credit card processing companies.

60%-70% lower fraud loss rates than other services.

Paypal also provides you a shopping cart that you can easily place directly on your website.

About 100 million active PayPal buyers worldwide.

Setup	Free
Orders By	Credit cards, PayPal
Transaction Fees	$0.30 + 1.9%-2.9%
Fee ($5/$20/$100 item)	$0.44/$0.88/$3.20

Payment to you is made into your bank account.

CCBill
This free credit card processing company only accepts customers who sell Web site content or services. It offers recurring billing and referral program.

Setup	Free
Orders By	Credit cards
Transaction Fees	14.5%
Fee ($5/$20/$100 item)	$0.73/$2.90/$14.50

Only issues checks.
CCBill holds 5% of the total revenues for a period of 26 weeks.
Payments every 7 days.

ClickBank

ClickBank accepts customers who offer digital products and services that are delivered entirely over the Internet itself (via Web pages, files, or email). Your products are promoted through their network of over 100,000 online affiliates. You select an affiliate commission percentage in advance.

Setup	$49.95
Orders By	Credit cards, debit cards, online checks
Transaction Fees	$1 + 7.5%
Fee ($5/$20/$100 item)	$1.38/$2.50/$8.50

Only issue checks. Charge $2.50 to process and send check.
Withhold 10% of each check which is released after about 90 days. Payments twice per month.

ShareIt!

This 3rd party credit card processing company helps you sell software and shareware via the Internet.

Setup	Free
Orders By	Credit cards, money orders, bank/wire transfer, check, cash
Transaction Fees	$2.95 + 5% or 14.9% but not less than $2.50
Fee ($5/$20/$100 item)	$2.50/$2.98/$7.95

You can choose between US Dollars, Euro and Pound Sterling for payment by bank transfer, check, or direct deposit in the USA. Fees for issuing monthly payments to you: Transfer to your account (bank transfer): $2 (Germany = free) Mailing a check: $5 (USA = free) Direct Deposit (USA only): free

CC Now

This credit card processor focuses on selling tangible merchandise that will be shipped to online shoppers.

Setup	$25
Orders By	Credit cards, PayPal
Monthly Cost	USA - $9.95 + 9% of your total sales in excess of $100.00 International - $11.95 + 11% of your total sales in excess of $100.00 (during the initial 30 day trial period you won't be charged a $9.95/$11.95 monthly fee)

They issue checks in US Dollars: $4.

Direct Deposit (USA only): free.

Wire Transfer: $40.

Reserve Funds are used if your length of sales history with CC Now is less than 3 months and sales earnings exceed $1000 in one semi-monthly pay period (see Web site for more details).

Payments twice per month (you can specify a payment threshold amount).

See Free Merchant Accounts for more information on the advantages and disadvantages of using 3rd party credit card processing companies.

Figure 13.1 ... Source: www.buildwebsite4u.com

What you risk reveals what you value.
- Jeanette Winterson

Alexa Software

This website www.alexa.com can help you check your site's popularity on the internet. It shows report on traffic statistics of websites (operating on the internet).

With Alexa, any webmaster can get hidden information about any website he/she visited online such as name of the site's owner, address, telephone number, email address etc. This information is important for those who want to go into online joint venture. So, you have to download this software (alexa) via www.alexa.com before you would be able to use it to get/gather undisclosed information on any website.

Ebook Cover Template

Ebook cover template could be created via any of these sites www.killercover.com and www.onlinewebcreations.com. If you have the skills, you may choose to design it yourself by using cover generating software. You can equally do a search on the internet via search engines for quality ebook cover templates.

Ebook Converter Software

Make sure your ebook is packaged in Portable Document Format (PDF) in order to prevent people making alterations to the content of the book. With Nitro PDF, Microsoft Word (MS Word 2007 and 2010) document could be converted into Portable document format (PDF).

Tracking Software (Article)

It is essential that you track your articles so as to prevent people making alterations to your signature file and your name. If you fail to track your articles (those you have submitted to article publishing sites), and someone alters the content of your resource box (which entails your name and other vital information), then your aim of driving traffic to your site via submission of article(s) to article publishing site(s) will not be achieved. Undoubtedly, your traffic (visitors) will be diverted to another site.

The beauty of tracking your article(s) is that, it gives you an opportunity to know where it is placed (or they are placed) on the internet. For this reason, it is important that you go to www.google.com/alert and set up an alert account that will enable you track your article. Moreover, you make sure that the title of each of your articles is indicated on the web form you are going to fill in on the internet. In addition, you ensure that you provide all the relevant information before you submit the form (online form)

Besides, you have to select web to enable Google send you report on articles that relate to the one (article) you published online.

After signing up for Google alert, you have to check your email box so as to confirm an alert message that Google will send to you. With that, whenever your article (or any of your articles) comes up on the internet, an alert email will be sent to you by Google. This will enable you check your article to see that it is not tampered with.

Ebook Compiler Software

This software is designed to prevent unauthorized access to information contained in your ebook. Getting ebook compiler software with quality features such as password protection, graphics, hyperlinks, survey(s) etc is essential for you.

Here are sites to visit for ebook compiler software:

http://www.pdf995.com
http://www.mindlikewater.com/ebook_software_publisher.html.

Other Internet Tools

There are lots of online tools (free or paid) that are not mentioned which you can use to get optimum business growth. For instance, article publishing software can help you submit articles to websites that accept same (articles) for publication. Also, there is an ad tracking software. This software is designed to help webmasters track their advertising campaigns in order to get optimal results for their efforts (otherwise they might be making unprofitable decisions if their ads are not tracked).

Suppose you were getting huge advertising clicks from Google.com to your site's home page via Google adwords {pay per click (PPC) advertising campaign} but low sales revenue as a result of few clicks you are getting from your site's home page link – that's the link that takes people from your home page to your sales page.

In the scenario above, the problem is not your PPC advertising campaign but rather your site's content (the content on your home page).

With this valuable information, you would be able to take a profitable decision by re-adjusting your website's content so as to attract more clicks.

Can you see the advantage of tracking your advertising campaign, now? So, the best way to avoid wasting money unknowingly is to track your advertising campaigns.

Please note that you can do a search on the internet via Google search, Yahoo! search, Bing or any other major search engines for any online tools that are not mentioned in this book. A lot of online tools (software) are there on the internet for your use (either free or paid).

You cannot have a successful business on the internet without traffic, so join me in the next chapter as I show you various techniques for driving traffic (people) to your website.

CHAPTER 14

ONLINE TRAFFIC GENERATION:
... Key To Online Business Success 1

http://www.clipartof.com/details/clipart/34918.html

Preamble

Your business success on the internet is mainly dependent on the traffic you are generating. If your website (business) is not generating considerable traffic (a reasonable number of visitors), then you cannot run a successful business on the internet. Making residual income on the internet is pivot (hinge) on considerable traffic your site is attracting.

Thus, before registering and hosting your domain name (website) through a web hosting company, a very critical issue you have to address is traffic - how to drive people to your site (get people attracted to your site). Having a website is useless if there is no traffic.

So, your site will earn nothing if nobody knows its presence on the internet.

That is simply the reason you have to take the issue of traffic very serious. Since your purpose of going online in the first place is to make money, then all your efforts must be geared to get people to visit your site on the internet.

On the internet, traffic is king. You earn nothing, if your site attracts no traffic (does not generate any traffic). You earn some money if you generate some traffic. However, with a huge amount of traffic you are sure of generating massive income.

Essentially, the nature of your online business (the one you are running at present or you intend to do) will determine whether you need traffic to succeed or not.

In actual fact, you don't need traffic to make money from surveys or data entry since you need not to create a website – your own website, before rendering these services. Obviously, these services could be rendered on the internet through a third party site (or third party sites).

However, if the nature of your business requires that you create a website (or perhaps you've already created one), then it is your responsibility to promote it if you hope to achieve your aim - boost your business profits.

Having known the importance of traffic (attracting huge traffic for that matter) to your online business, it is about time you read this essential chapter and the next (chapter 15). These two chapters are written to show you various avenues of attracting traffic to your site.

Undoubtedly, your success on the internet is determined by the number of people visiting your site.

So, it is essential that you use some of the marketing techniques – online and offline, you are going to read in this book to drive visitors (people) to your site.

In fact, if you need a website that works – either personal or corporate website, do not hesitate to contact me via +234-702-7098213 & www.online-business-success-tips.blogspot.com for special (one-on-one) internet consulting services. I will help you (or your company) build a profitable online business rather than just host a website.

Traffic Generation #1: Online Article Marketing

One of the powerful and pungent ways of promoting sites on the internet is article marketing. Article marketing is all about publishing an article with the aim of attracting traffic to a site. You send article (or articles) to article publishing website(s) {site(s) that accept articles from webmasters for publication on the internet}. You may forward one or two articles a week (probably a month) to article publishing site(s) with the aim of driving traffic to your site.

The article publishing websites in turn make these articles available free of charge to people (webmasters, newsletter publishers etc.) who use them as content on their websites. While it's free to use these articles, the users are not allowed to alter any of the articles – neither the content nor the signature file (signature file normally appears at the bottom of an article). A well prepared signature file will attract traffic to your site. So, in order to achieve your aim of driving people to your site through article marketing, you make sure that your signature file is well packaged (the same for the content of your article).

It is, therefore, essential that you write a powerful (attention grabbing) signature file. Your signature file should entail your name, e-mail address, phone number, and any vital information that will make people to visit your site.

> **Often attitudes are kindled in the flame of others' convictions. - Louis E. Le Bar**

Guidelines to Article Marketing

1. Ensure that your article is related to the content of your site, but not the same as your site's content to avoid your site being penalized.
2. You can come up with a quality article and a well packaged signature file through a thorough search on e-zine websites.
3. Endeavour to edit an article written or packaged by a ghost writer before submitting it.
4. You may use software to submit your articles to many e-zine sites (you need to do a search for that software).
5. Make your article(s) attractive with quality and fresh information in order to attract traffic (a large number of visitors) to your site.

These are some of the websites where you can submit your articles:

http://www.GoArticles.com
http://www.EzineArticles.com
http://www.ArticleCity.com
http://www.Isnare.com
http://www.Ideamarketers.com
http://www.ArticleCentral.com

http://www.ArticleHub.com
http://www.ArticleWarehouse.com
http://www.AuthorConnection.com
http://www.Zongoo.com
http://www.ContentDesk.com
http://www.Article-Emporium.com
http://www.ArticleHub.com
http://www.ReprintArticles.com

http://www.FreeGoogleTrafficSystem.com – this particular website helps you to discover various ways of attracting traffic to your site.

Traffic Generation #2: Forum Marketing

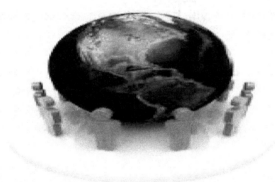

Source:http://www.mlmrecruitingonline.com/wp-content/uploads/2009/02/j0438475.jpg&imgrefurl

Getting your website out through forum marketing will add to your bottom line. This is another powerful way of getting traffic to your website. The first is to join a forum site that relates to your site's concept (where people who share identical opinions that relate to your niche market come together – to send and respond to issues). After that see how you can get people attracted to your site, through your signature file, as you respond to post frequently (always respond to issues with your signature file below your post).

Some members of the forum will, time after time, post information that relates to the content on your forum site (the forum site you set up account with) with the expectation that some other members of the forum would respond to them. Also, this information (content on the forum site you joined) ought to relate to your own site's content.

You can drive traffic to your site (get people to visit your own site) from a forum site without paying for advert. All you need to do is respond to issues, and make sure your signature file (which entails your website address, business slogan, and any information you think is important) appears at the bottom of your post (any of your responses). Definitely, some of the forum's members will be attracted to your site through this marketing technique.

See underneath a sample of signature file:

Your name: First and last name (or your surname)
The address of your site: www.yourdomainname.com (URL)
Email address: xxxx@yahoo.com (this is an example)
Your slogan: ... get IT training anywhere you are (this is an example)

Your signature file could appear at the bottom of any post you wish to reply to without typing it each time you respond to an issue (post) when you put it on your forum site's profile (provided you are permitted to do so by the owner of the forum site you have registered with).

You can send message(s), and equally respond to issues raised by other members of the forum site you have account with. In addition, ensure that you register with forum website(s) that have current information –

these are sites that post current and fresh information (not outdated information).

You should be looking for forum site(s) with huge numbers of subscriber base, say 2,000 and above; after all, your purpose of signing up should be to attract traffic to your site.

You make sure that your responses (or perhaps questions) are related to your site's content. Do not ruin your reputation by posting content that is not related to the forum site you've registered with. Additionally, ensure that you adhere strictly to the laid down rules of this site. So, make sure you do things in a polite manner.

You can even create a forum on your own site in an attempt to drive people to it. However, forum marketing is not without its own downside. The downside of forum marketing is that some of your members are bound to complain (and even tell some people about it) if they are not getting the desired results – that is your services/products are not up to standard. If this kind of problem comes up after creating a forum on your site, your reputation will be tarnished.

The foregoing paragraph must be seriously considered before creating a forum on your site so as not to ruin your reputation (or your business). So, think twice!

To get a forum site that relates to your niche market, you have to do a search on the internet via search engines such as Google, Yahoo! Search, Bing etc. by typing your niche market keyword and forum (if your keyword is **fish farming** for example, then you type **fish farming forum**) and then click on search button. The results of your searched keyword will be displayed thereafter.

Traffic Generation #3: Viral Marketing

Viral marketing is another avenue of getting people to visit your website. Viral marketing is a marketing strategy that is contagious like a virus, though not destructive.

With viral marketing, you can drive a huge number of visitors to your site by giving away valuable materials such as ebook, software etc. Since people naturally love free things, they will be willing to give you their email addresses so as to get these free goodies.

All you need to do is prepare a bundle of free materials you want to give away to your prospects, and upload them to your site. However, you make sure you get their names and email addresses before they are able to access these free stuff/materials.

You may instruct your prospects/customers to give away the same materials or sell them to their own subscribers at quoted prices - the prices you want the products (the free stuff) to be sold. Obviously, this is a sure way of driving traffic to your site.

We don't grow unless we take
risks. Any successful company
is riddled with failures.
- James E. Burke

As they keep visiting your site by virtue of your repeat free stuff, some will become your customers – even your life-long customers.

Giving free stuff to people will enhance your mailing list. The bottom line is that you will be able to sell back-end products to your customers in the future. Anytime you have a product you think will appeal to the minds of your customers, just send an email to intimate to them your new product. With this, you will be able to cash in a reasonable amount of money – that is the beauty of creating a mailing list.

Make sure your free ebook contains a link – an affiliate link (or your own website link), that directs people to your affiliate merchant's site (or your own website). As they click on this link, they are directed in a jiffy to your affiliate merchant's site (or your own site). Sooner or later, some of your subscribers (subscribers to your free ebook) will buy your affiliate's product (or your own site's product).

Traffic Generation #4: Blog Marketing

You may set up a blog for your Google adsense programme rather than a website since it is easier to promote a blog than a website. Naturally, every blog contains features that make it interactive and easy to promote [these features include asking question(s) and commenting on other people's opinions (issues)]. By virtue of these features, it is essential that you use blog for your Google adsense programme.

Tips for Marketing Your Blog

1. You make sure that you ping your blog whenever a post is made. With this site www.pingomatic.com, your ping (short high ringing sound) will be sent to blog directories at once to notify the directories of your new post.
2. You can equally use this website www.onlywire.com to get all your bookmarks sent at once. It is important that you bookmark your comments and your questions – you posted on the forum site, and

also ensure that your questions and responses (comments) are related to your blog's content.

3. To get your feeds listed on www.feedster.com directories so that people can sign up for it before they even come to your blog make sure you burn it with the site above.

4. To drive traffic to your blog you need to post comments (endeavour to add your blog's URL to your resource box) on other people's blogs.

5. In addition, make sure you update your blog regularly, and endeavour to post comments at least once a week. That is a sure way of getting people to visit your blog. You can use auto poster software for your blog update.

Check out this site www.auto-blog-feeder.com for fresh content on your blog if you are a wordpress user.

You can visit the site below as well
www.click-here-for.info/on/linkvine

Traffic Generation #5: Video Marketing

Through video websites such as Yahoo video, YouTube, Google video, video recording of your product etc., you can drive traffic (visitors) to your website, and subsequently profit from your visitors - selling your product(s) to them.

With recording tools such as video camera and video capturing software, you can capture all the activities appearing on your computer.

Video camera, for instance, can record an event that shows people how to use a particular product. After capturing this event, you have to save it on your computer system, and subsequently upload same to your website.

You can as well use video capturing software (Camtasia for example) to capture any activities you want people to see in the video on your computer such as ebook template, website graphics etc., then put the same on your computer, and thereafter upload it to your site.

Furthermore, you ensure that the quality of your video is high, and its content (the content on your video) is related to your site's concept.

http://www.masternewmedia.org/images/buzz_480.jpg &imgrefurl

When you are through with the video recording, the next is to subscribe to one or more video websites, and upload your video file(s) to the sites you have registered with. However, you make sure that your signature file is created on your video site's profile page – for people to look at. You may even watermark (with a special software) your website address on your video in order to register it (your website address) in the minds of your visitors as they watch the video clip of your product on the internet.

Ensure that a brief description of your video contains your site's content and your website address. You have to make your video clip short so as not to take much time – value your prospect's time.

You can visit any video websites on the internet to view videos you can use on your site without creating your own video clip – paid or free video clip. Make sure the clip is related to your site's content.

As soon as you get a free video clip (if you are able to get one) on the internet, via any of the search engines, that relates to your site's concept, all you need to do is play the video by clicking on the start button, and then click on embed. In seconds, a code will appear on your monitor screen, copy and paste it anywhere you want the video to emerge on your webpage.

Mind you, you have to create a descriptive keyword (related to your site's concept) for this video and ensure that the video web page is listed on search engines.

With this, you will be able to drive people to your website. Moreover, if you want people to keep visiting your site, you have to update it (your site) at regular time – of course with invaluable content.

You can use the same method to create audio clip on your website, and still drive people to it (your website). You may even attract more clicks with audio clips than the video. Nevertheless, you still have to write an attractive description of your audio keyword(s).

You may visit the website below for video web wizard software that will help you upload video clips on your website within a reasonable short time –

http://www.sixbucks.com/prod7may31/proda/index.html

Traffic Generation #6: Social Networking

You can also drive traffic to your website through social networking sites such as twitter and face book. All you need to do is register with these sites - it does not cost you anything (subscription is free) to register with them.

After signing up, you have to create a signature file which you are going to use to attract traffic to your site. Don't forget that your signature file should entail your website address, and it must be placed on your social networking site's profile so that your followers can view it.

Moreover, it is essential that you follow up your followers – visit their pages, so that they in turn can visit your profile page (where you placed your signature file); and subsequently your site as they click on your site address that is placed on your profile page.

See this piece of information below from Wikipedia:
Twitter is a free social networking and micro-blogging service that enables its users to send and read messages known as "tweets". Tweets are text-based posts of up to 140 characters displayed on the author's profile page and delivered to the author's subscribers who are known as followers.

Senders can restrict delivery to those in their circle of friends or, by default, allow open access. Users can send and receive tweets via the Twitter website, Short Message Service (SMS) or external applications. While the service costs nothing to use, accessing it through SMS may incur phone service provider fees.

Tips to Getting Traffic from Social Networking Site:

1. By getting new twitter's friends to follow up on a regular basis you will drive traffic to your site.
2. Send tweets to your followers (fans) regularly, and endeavour to respond promptly to their tweets (your followers' tweets)
3. As you sign up with many social networking sites more visitors will be attracted to your site.
4. Indeed, you can get a huge number of visitors to your site from social networking sites while you are on the hunt for new friends to follow up on social networking sites - sites that pull lots of traffic on a regular basis.
5. Moreover, you ought to know the reason why you visit these sites – social networking sites such as face book, twitter etc., so that you don't get trapped in the fun. It is essential that you have a time schedule so that you know when to logon and to sign out before using any of the social networking sites.

Vision gives you the impulse
to make the picture your own.
- Robert Collier

You can visit this site to enhance your traffic generation (from twitter) http://www.six-bucks.com/prod9jun15

Traffic Generation #7: Social Bookmarking

These are sites that help subscribers (those that signed up with them) bookmark their favourite sites. These subscribers often share their favourite sites with other users of the bookmarking sites. Bookmarking sites are sites with huge numbers of people visiting them on a daily basis.

You will see a list of social bookmarking sites you can register with as you click on the hyperlinks (shown on the screen) one after the other (in separate window or tab) - after you have signed up with www.onlywire.com (though you still have to logon to your account on www.onlywire.com before gaining access to this list).

When you are through with your registration with any of the social bookmarking sites, you have to come back to this site www.onlywire.com and enter the usernames and passwords (if they are not the same) you used at the time of registering with the social bookmarking sites (or enter your username and password if you have account with only one bookmarking site). Subsequently, you click on save button to save this information (usernames and passwords) on www.onlywire.com.

As you click on onlywire icon on your computer screen with a mouse (onlywire.com icon must first of all be placed on your toolbar before you can view it on your computer screen), you will be directed to this site www.onlywire.com. As soon as you get there, then supply the relevant keywords for this web page [these are keywords that relate to a webpage on onlywire.com]. Additionally, ensure all the necessary information that appears on the screen is equally supplied before clicking on submit button.

You do exactly the same for other web pages on your site (including the pages you are going to add to your site in the future). After that, the bookmarks and the keywords you entered on your site's webpages are automatically sent by www.onlywire.com to all the social bookmarking sites you've signed up with.

Any time a member of any of these social bookmarking sites types (as he/she conducts a search for information on the internet) a keyword that relates to your site's concept, your website appears forthwith. This is one of the ways of attracting traffic to your website.

Furthermore, to increase the number of people that come to your site you have to tell your friends, relatives etc. to add your web page to their favourite social bookmarking sites. You can also use your website to pass the same message (tell people to add your site to their favourite bookmarking sites) to other people. Obviously, this traffic generating technique will add to your bottom line!

Traffic Generation #8: Search Engine Optimization (SEO)

Natural search traffic is a traffic that costs you nothing to generate – you don't have to pay a dime. Your site will certainly attract natural search traffic on a search engine if found among the top twenty web links (the first two web pages on notable search engines for keyword that relates to your site) as someone searches for a keyword that relates to your site's concept.

Search Engine Optimization (SEO) is broadly divided into two – off-site and on-site. When your website gets visitors through inbound link(s) such traffic is regarded as off-site traffic, but the traffic that comes through search engines is known as on-site traffic.

Inbound links (links that come from other websites such as forum sites, social networking sites, auction sites etc other than search engines such as Google, Yahoo! Search, Bing etc.) are created to enhance site's traffic. However, for inbound links to be valuable to any search engines they have to come from important websites – a top ranking sites on search engines and low ranking on Alexa.com. Your site will turn out to be a top ranking site (or one of the top ranking sites) on www.google.com and any other notable search engines if it has many inbound links.

You can also get links by taking part in N-way link exchange service – you don't need a webmaster to exchange link with. Visit the sites below for details:
www.1waylinks.net
www.3waylinks.net
www.mywaylinks.com

However, it is essential that you don't direct all your links to your home page. You need to direct them to different pages on your site if you don't want the search engines to become suspicious. Moreover, you have to build your inbound links slowly.

For on-site SEO, the HTML code must be cleaned – putting Java Script code and style sheet code separately will help.

Other guidelines to getting search engine optimization (SEO) recognition are as follows (for on-site SEO):

1 Don't use another website's content on your own website to avoid duplicating the content
2 Having internal links (links within a website) is good for search engine ranking. Please note that linking words like "here" or "click here" will do your site no good. Since these words are not recognized by the search engines so it will not add to your bottom line. Therefore, it is worthwhile to use a descriptive keyword. For instance, for penny stock (as a keyword), you may use "penny stock analysis".
3 Create a website map you can link to all the pages on your site. You can use Google tool to create it.
4 Make sure your keywords are typed in bold. Heading1 and heading2, as shown in Microsoft Word

toolbar, should be used for your title and your subtitle.

5 Finally, your keywords should appear on your web page's title position (title tag).

Traffic Generation #9: Google Adwords

Google adwords is another avenue of generating traffic to your website, though not a free ad campaign. That means you have to pay Google before using this marketing technique to drive traffic to your site.

Source: __http://training.seobook.com/google-ranking-value__ (for Google Adwords and SEO)

> ### *There is no more miserable human being than one in whom nothing is habitual but indecision.*
> ### *- William James*

The amount of money Google charges an advertiser (someone who placed sponsored ad on Google) for a click on a sponsored ad is hugely dependent on the keyword and the bidding price the advertiser could afford to pay. However, if you sign up for Google adwords programme your account will be credited with money (amount deposited). You will also be credited with some amount of money if you take part in survey programme.

Websites are positioned (ranked) - after such have been listed on the search engine - on Google.com based on the amount of money [for pay per click (PPC)] each one of the bidders is willing to pay for a click emanating from the search engine - where the sponsored ads are placed. Advertisers often enter a competition (bidding) so as to determine which of the sites (advertisers' sites) gets the first spot, and the other positions in descending order on the same search engine for a specific keyword. Thus, an advertiser that enters the highest bid for a specific keyword (or phrase) gets the first spot (his ad is placed at the top), while the second highest bidder for same keyword gets the second spot. Of course, the lowest bidder occupies the last spot.

Therefore, the bidding price an advertiser is willing to pay for PPC advertising campaign will determine the position of his advert. Surely, if someone clicks on the sponsored ad placed on this search engine, the advertiser's adwords account (for PPC ad campaign) will be deducted forthwith.

Traffic Generation #10: Bulk SMS Marketing

You can use short message service (SMS) – bulk SMS marketing to attract traffic to your website. All you need to do is use any of the search engines to search for companies that render bulk SMS service on the internet.

After that, you set up a bulk SMS account with a company (SMS service provider) you have a strong preference for (and subsequently pay for the number of SMS you need), and there after advertise your products and your website via text messages to your prospects and your customers alike.

You can set up a bulk SMS account with this website www.bulksmsportal.com

Traffic Generation #11: Newsletter Marketing

Another name for newsletter marketing is email marketing, and it is another means of generating traffic. You can use this method to drive traffic to your site by sending periodic newsletter to your prospects and customers alike (even sell back-end products to your customers).

Many of life's failures are men who did not realize how close they were to success when they gave up.
- Thomas Edison

Tips for getting people to open and read your newsletter

- ✓ Make sure the subject of your newsletter grabs your prospects (an attractive title will make them open your newsletter)
- ✓ Explore the internet for a subject title that is attractive to your prospects or research into your local newspapers for same
- ✓ Let the headline of your email or newsletter reveals what the newsletter is all about. Merely reading the headline your prospects should be able to discern that the newsletter is yours.
- ✓ Do not give your prospects false information – don't deceive them for whatever reason
- ✓ Put your name in the FROM LINE so that your prospects will know where the email is coming from
- ✓ If you are sending email to a prospect (not all your subscribers), make sure you personalize it by putting the name of the recipient in the email subject line
- ✓ You can create conversation with your prospects if your current newsletter is a continuation of your previous discussion (previous newsletter) with them`
- ✓ Finally, in order to get optimal results from your subject headline, send two subject headlines (two different topics) to a group of people on your mailing list, say hundred (100) people. The results of this text will help you determine which of the subject headlines is appropriate (and profitable) for you, and the headline to chuck out. As soon as you identify the headline that is profitable to you (or appropriate for you), send the same newsletter (your profitable headline) to your customers and prospects alike (to all your subscribers) after reviewing it.

Traffic Generation #12: E-zine Ad, Classified Ad, Banner Ad & Renting Email

By using free or/and paid ad(s) you can attract traffic to your site. The ads include classified, online banners and links to complementary sites.

Classified ad

You can place a classified ad (a piece of information) on some classified ad websites to drive people to your site. It could be paid or free advert.

For classified ads, visit the following websites
www.buysellbid.com
www.freeclassifiedlinks.com

Banner ad

Banner advertisement (ad) comes in the form of a graph and rectangular in shape. It always conveys advertising information, and it can be displayed on a website in order to attract traffic to another website (example, y\our website).

For a free banner exchange visit www.buildtrafficx.com

Link to complementary sites

You can also link your site to websites (other people's websites) that sell complementary products (sites that are not selling/rendering the same products/services as yours). Site that sells cell phones can exchange link with a telecommunication company (website) that offers telephone services. It is worthwhile to use this kind of **ad** campaign for your Google adsense programme.

www.free-ezine-directory.com

E-zine ads

E-zine ads are usually placed on newsletters that are periodically sent to prospects and customers alike.

These ads are placed close to the content on the newsletter (on the right, left or top side). An e-zine ad will attract traffic (visitors) to your site if such (advertisement) is captivating.

www.directoryofezine.com

Renting email list
You can buy a mailing list that relates to your niche market in order to drive people to your site. The downside of this is that you are more likely to get SPAM (unsolicited emails).

www.buyerzone.com
www.yesmail.com

Traffic Generation #13: Free Online Public Relation

You can visit these sites for online public relation tips
www.xpresspress.com
www.marketwire.com

Traffic Generation #14: Affiliate Marketing

Affiliate marketing is another potent marketing technique that people normally employ to create customers for their products and to build mailing lists (to sell back-end products in the future).

You (an individual or a company) start by placing advert on a website that runs free or paid advertising campaign. As people visit this site (where your ad is being run) and click on your captivating ad, they will be directed forthwith to your autoresponder where both their names and email addresses would be captured (collected).

Forthwith, the autoresponder (after capturing their names and email addresses) sends sales copy (containing an affiliate hotlink or hyperlink) of your product to these prospects in an attempt to direct them to your merchant's site (where the product will be bought).

> *The wise man bridges the gap*
> *by laying out the path by*
> *means of which he can get*
> *from where he is to where he*
> *wants to go.*
> *- John Pierpont Morgan*

Aside the above, you ensure that you follow up these prospects regularly via your autoresponder.

With a thorough follow up some prospects would become your customers by virtue of purchasing your product. In addition to this, you can also use your mailing list to drive people to your own website (if you have a website or create one in the future) via a sales copy whenever you have a back-end product to sell. What a wonderful way to get people to visit your site (your own site) via a mailing list!

Join me in chapter 15 as I show you how offline traffic generating techniques will complement your efforts in chapter 14. The bottom line is that you get more people to visit your website.

CHAPTER 15

OFFLINE TRAFFIC GENERATION:
... Key To Online Business Success 2

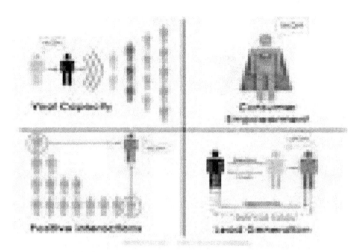

http://www.intersectionconsulting.com/blog/wp
-content/uploads/2009/04/wom-
500p.jpg&imgrefurl

Preamble

Aside generating traffic via the internet, you can as well drive people to your online business through the newspaper advertisements, even tell people about your online business or give them (people) your website address (this is called Word of mouth marketing) etc. These are just some of the ways (offline) of generating traffic to your site.

Since traffic is essential to your online business success, you have to harness every possible means – online and offline marketing strategies (either free and/or paid marketing campaigns), to get your website out (to drive traffic to your site). Really, this chapter is written to complement your online traffic generating efforts.

Traffic Generation #1: Word of Mouth Marketing

Source:http://wildpitchmarketing.com/wpcontent/uploads/2010/04/word-of-mouth-marketing.jpg&imgrefurl

You can tell people about the presence of your website using the "word of mouth marketing". This is one of the marketing strategies that get your site out. You give people your website address (also tell them the products/services you are offering for sale) so as to visit it (your website).

If you had explored the internet prior to this time, you would have discovered that a keyword via Google search could generate millions of pages. So, if you don't promote your site people would not know its presence, and they won't visit it, and invariably won't attract any click. Therefore, it is important that you make people aware of the existence of your website through word of mouth marketing (you need to get people to visit your site through this marketing technique).

Word of mouth marketing makes it possible for people to visit your website (or blog) as you give them your site address (and encouraging them to visit it). With this marketing strategy, you will find out in no distant time that your website is attracting some clicks as you engage people, apart from yourself, to help you publicize your website address (your website URL).

You can give away your company's promotional materials such as prospectus, hand bills, posters etc. Ensure that these materials entail the name of your company, office address, email address, the products you are offering, your website address, and of course, any vital information (contact information such as telephone number) that will promote your site.

Traffic Generation #2: Free Offline Article Marketing

If you have flair for writing, you can write and submit articles to print media that relates to your niche market. All you need to do is get a news editor you could forward your articles and your covering letter to.

Endeavour to follow up these documents (your articles and your covering letter) with an email or a phone call to ensure that the person got them. You might even get a column in the same newspaper after a short time. Offline article marketing is another great way of promoting your site as you include your resource box at the bottom of each one of your articles.

Choose always the way that seems the best, however rough it may be. Custom will soon render it easy and agreeable. - Pythagoras

Traffic Generation #3: Free Offline Public Relation

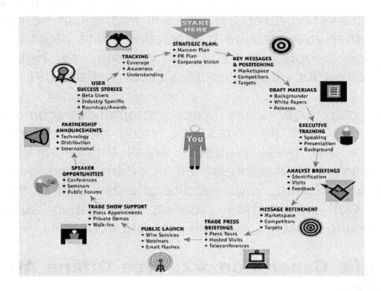

http://www.frontpagepr.com/images/steps_in_the_proc ess.gif&imgrefurl

Another great way of attracting people to your site is through offline public relation. If you have the privilege to talk to a reporter of a print media, local radio or television station about an important issue that relates to your expertise or your niche market; it is indeed, a great way of publicizing your website, and invariably attracting traffic to it.

Traffic Generation #4: Paid Offline Advertisement

Aside online advertising campaign, you can also get your site out through paid offline advertisement – so that people can visit it. So, you have to pay a sum of money to get your products/services (and of course, your website) advertised in any print media that relates to your niche market.

You simply have to look for a print media with a huge number of subscriber base (thousands of readers for instance) such as "The Punch" newspaper, Guardian etc., and place your advertisement there. You may as well place your advertisement (to advertise your website) in any newspaper or magazine that publishes information relating to your niche market. Whichever print media you choose to do business with, you have to take into account the advertising expenses.

Traffic Generation #5: Telephone Marketing

http://cdn.trak.in/wp-content/uploads/2008/04/mobile-phone-usage.jpg&imgrefurl

You can use your cell phone to call your existing customers. This will create a strong relationship between you and them (your customers). With that, they will keep you in mind. The bottom line is that you get some of your customers making repeat orders, and this will invariably increase your profits.

You may use the same marketing strategy to reach your prospects – those that have not bought your products/services even though they signed up for your newsletter (though initial contacts were established). Through telephone marketing, some of your prospects might become your customers (even life-long customers).

> ### *Obstinacy in opinions holds the dogmatist in the chains of error, without the hope of emancipation.*
> ### *- John C. Granville*

Traffic Generation #6: Get Your Website Known

Putting your website address, email address(es) in your business prospectus, business card, stickers, wedding gifts, print book (hard copy) – if you have authored one, letter head papers, offline banners, posters, hand bills, tee shirts or anything that can promote your website in this brick and mortal world (any of these can drive traffic to your site). Anything that will promote your website put your site link there, even your answering machine if you have one. Anything! Anything!! Anything!!!

In the next chapter, you will learn how to choose the best money-making techniques that are appropriate for you.

CHAPTER 16

OPTING FOR ONLINE BUSINESSES THAT FIT YOU

http://mr-crocker.deviantart.com/art/I-Am-A-Happy-Person-4736843

Start with Your Skills (Talents)

This book has shown you various ways of creating income on the internet – from info product to incentive offers, but you must understand that you don't have to engage yourself in all the twelve income streams. Apparently, you won't fit into all, so you have to decide which of the income streams are best suited for you.

Considering the fact that you don't have the natural ability to do all these money making activities superbly, it is therefore essential that you focus on activities you have passion for – activities that you like very much.

When you focus on money making activities you have flair for (activities you have passionate interest in) you are going to succeed because you are doing what you most enjoy.

Just do what you do best.
- Red Auerbach

For instance, if you have flair for writing, you should focus on online income streams 1, 3, 9 and probably 4. With superb writing communication skills, you can set up an online business in diverse areas such as creating online course, rendering investment tips via newsletter, writing business plan (if you are a financial consultant), making money through Google adsense etc. A marketing professional should focus on online income streams 2, 4 (rendering marketing consulting services), 8, 9, 10 and 12.

Computer engineering consultant can build a business around online income streams 4 (rendering computer engineering consulting services) and 11.

If you have a business – an offline business, the best you can do is to take the same (your business) to the internet, rather than setting up another business (a new business) online. However, you may add one or more online money making techniques (already revealed in this book) to your offline business so as to enhance your revenue.

If you render financial consulting services offline for instance, you could create an online presence of this business (to complement your offline business). With a website, you can give financial advice to people via newsletter on a specific niche market such as "how to manage a successful business", "how to boost your annual sales revenue by 100% etc.

If you are a teacher, you can use e-zine to improve students' learning skills (or build an e-zine business around any subject that interests you). You can explore the internet for valuable information that will enhance the quality of your newsletters. Of course, you have the potential to make money on the internet. You have something to impart to other people – something that people could pay for. That is it!

All you need to do is discover the skills, talents, knowledge etc that you have – something you can impart to people and get paid for it. Any services you could sell to people. You can build a business around whatever skills you possess. A lot of people are looking for a way out of their problems. If you think out of the box, you will discover something (knowledge) people can pay for.

Focusing on your core business – your offline business, on the internet is the best decision (if you have a well established offline business); though you may add some money making techniques such as info products, affiliate marketing etc., depending on your capability, to your core offline business. This will help you to exhibit the same skills and knowledge (experience) you've got over the years. So, you don't have to start a new business – start to learn new things (aside the knowledge that will help you to operate efficiently and effectively on the internet such as internet marketing, traffic generating techniques etc. – these will add to your bottom line).

If you think through, you will discover something (concepts/ideas) to profit from on the internet. You might even realize you could render some services (impart knowledge to people) online which you have never envisaged.

Whatever business (even if you are selling hard/physical products such as computers, motor vehicles, electronics etc.) you are doing at present, you can take it online in order to enhance your revenue. You might even discover how to do something in a better way on the internet.

Do What You Have Passion for and Be Passionate about It

Are you a newbie? Are you in a dilemma – you don't know which of the online money-making streams to choose from? You could be successful in making money on the internet if you have passion for what you intend to do (or what you are doing). If you are passionate about what you intend to do (or you do) online, you are going to work with less effort because you are doing what you most enjoy. If you have flair for figures, build an online business around it – help people to solve their mathematical problems.

If you are good at writing article, for instance, make money from it - you can venture into e-zine business. You could also profit from info products.

Do you love taking pictures with your camera? Why don't you cash in money from this (endeavour to read chapter 6)? Of course, you can build an online business around it - around your hobbies (or whatever skills you possess).

Are you an artist? Do you know you can market your art on the internet and make money from it?

> ### The biggest mistake people make in life is not making a living at doing what they most enjoy.
> ### - Malcolm S. Forbes (1919-1990)

However, before you venture into any online business, make sure you do your home work– have a thorough plan for your online business. If you fail to plan you are most likely to fail. So, before setting up your online business, get to know what will make it (business) succeed and do exactly that.

Setting up a business is one thing, making a success of it is another thing. Thus, you need to figure out how to make your business stand out in the crowd if you really want to make headway. This is peculiar to a niche market with many companies selling (rendering) the same products (services), and there is intense competition.

Getting first-rate and unique information – information that is fresh and attractive - will drive traffic to your website in thousands, and your business will stand out.

It is therefore necessary that you take a considerable amount of time for proper planning. **Don't rush to launch out your online business in order not to run out.** Take your time ... and make a clued-up (well-informed) decision before you launch out.

You should know that it takes time to build a business - either online or offline. Therefore do not expect money to start coming in a week or two - though it is not impossible.

Additionally, you must understand that you cannot leave your business to chance because success does not come that way. You can only achieve success through persistent and positive attitude (put up your best – let your mind be there, and think positively).

So, with a proper planning, positive mindset, determination and perseverance, and making use of the right tools, you are sure of building a lucrative online business.

Though it may take you months or few years to create a profitable business on the internet, but success is guaranteed if you do the right things (if you follow the rules).

I hope you will have something to learn from the story below.

Claudia & Dave Nelson's Blog Information is power, but without applied wisdom it can be of no use.

Posted on August 25, 2010 by Dave

I want you to understand something about me, and from this day forward, I want you to take a long hard look at yourself and decide what it is that you REALLY want out of life because you've got to make a choice

You either do what you need to, or you don't... There is no middle ground. No, "have your cake and eat it".

You see, I'm not intelligent by society's standard. It took me 5 years to graduate from college with a 2.0 and my newsletters have more spelling errors than Paris Hilton has boyfriends.

I took all of my finance classes, all of my accounting classes, and all of my math classes THREE TIMES EACH, before I passed them.

But I was smart enough to know a few things that most people don't... I knew there was no "we'll do it for you" solution to anything in life.

I knew I needed to master a few key skill sets if I was to get what I wanted, which is why I spent most of my college years, not in class, but at Barne's and Noble reading "real" books on business.

I knew that if I wanted to stop buying leads, I'd need to learn how to generate my own, so I bought some books and learned how.

I knew that if I wanted to sell my business and products to people, that I'd need to learn how to write a sales letter, so I
bought some books and learned how.

I knew that if I wanted to make my own sales letters, I'd need to learn how to make a website, so I bought some books and learned how.

I knew that if I wanted to be successful in networking, I'd need to get over my fear of the phone, so I took a job that required me to make 200-300 cold calls per day, and learned how.

But here's the one thing I NEVER DID during the past 6 years that allowed me to go from "Point A to Point Rich…"

I never complained, I never whined, I never bitched, I never blamed anyone other than myself, and I never gave up because I would have rather spent my life in poverty trying, than to have lived in resignation that I didn't have what it took.

I don't want to burst your bubble, but here's God's Honest Truth…

If you want what I've got, you've got to be willing to do what I've done.

You've got to earn the right through sweat, and tears, and there is NO alternative, so don't ever ask me or anyone else if there's an "easy way" to do something.

Are you willing to do that?

Shared with you by: David W Nelson

Author of www.JoinDavidWNelson.com

www.claudia-dave-nelsonblog.com

Go to the next chapter for tips that get you started.

Chapter 17

GETTING STARTED RIGHT AWAY...

http://shelleytherepublican.com/category/gtrat-deals

Having discovered the various ways of making money on the internet, and how to choose the best money making technique(s) that is/are suitable for you from a wide range of options, it is high time you started to ...

> *Knowing is not enough;*
> *we must apply. Willing is*
> *not enough; we must do.*
> *– Johann von Goethe*

After choosing your niche market and the products/services you want to sell – something you love and have passion for (endeavour to read chapter 16 thoroughly), you need to get connected to the internet right away and set up a website (or a blog if you wish).

Next, fill your site with quality and fresh content (or whatever products you are offering), and get all the needed online tools for starting-off; and finally apply some of the techniques for driving traffic (you have learned) to your site. These are the essential things you have to do to get started...

As you apply some of the traffic generating techniques (in chapters 14 and 15 of this book), and keep providing your visitors with fresh and quality content (coupled with some inbound links – links coming from quality sites to your own website), expect your website to grow in traffic, and subsequently in money.

Therefore, as you do what you love the money will come. However, you may have to wait for some time before you start to make money with your site. So you've got to be patient.

Come visit me at **www.online-business-success-tips.blogspot.com** for special (one-on-one) online business consulting services on how to build a profitable internet business (a website that works and generates residual income). You can as well reach me via +234-702-709-8213 or +234-805-546-6759.

I wish you the best on your journey to financial breakthrough. **Be blessed**!

> *Developing the plan is actually laying out the sequence of events that have to occur for you to achieve your goal.*
> *- George L. Morrisey*

The page is intentionally left blank

Special Consulting Services

- ✓ Underground secrets of boosting your annual business revenue (virtually all small businesses) by 100% or more revealed...
- ✓ No matter what your profession, occupation or business (even if you are without a job) is, I will show you how to **generate residual income** (to enhance your earnings) on the internet - to build **your own profitable online business** (not just build a website) around your hobbies, skills, talents, experience etc. If you are interested, please call +234(0)702-709-8213 or +234(0)805-546-6759.
- ✓ Are you willing to discover **some lucrative business ideas** (**DO IT YOURSELF** investments) you could venture into to change your financial situation for better? If your answer is YES, then contact me via 009-234(0)702-709-8213 or 009-234(0)805-546-6759

Come visit me at **www.online-business-success-tips.blogspot.com.** You can equally send email to robest2007@gmail.com

Please, text or send ***free marketing tip, your name, your telephone number, your email address and your comment on what you have gained from this book*** to **+234(0)805-546-6759** or **robest2007@gmail.com** for a free marketing tip that will boost your income (revenue).

*Defeat never comes to any
man until he admits it.
- Josephus Daniels*

www.ingramcontent.com/pod-product-compliance
Lightning Source LLC
Chambersburg PA
CBHW071422050326
40689CB00010B/1937